Colonel Harris has drawn upon his experience as an Army officer and his qualification in workplace health and safety matters in this complete dissertation upon Pony Club Mounted Games. He traces the introduction of Prince Philip Mounted Games in Australia, his family's involvement and his progress from a non-horsey parent to a horseman, rider, competitor, coach and mentor of Pony Club squads and teams, and qualification under the National Coaches Accreditation Scheme.

For a number of years David Harris has been the coach of the New South Wales Pony Club Mounted Games Squad and coach of the state team. He has also been coach of the Pony Club Australia international teams to Canada and the United Kingdom.

This book is full of invaluable information to coaches and parents regarding the selection and training of the mounted games pony; to coaches and riders on the riding skills required for mounted games generally and the particular techniques to carry out the various types of movements in the individual games. It covers everything one would wish to know about the conduct of mounted games and is an easy-to-read handbook. The explanations are clear and the photographs helpful.

Books abound in the other riding disciplines. This book fills a gap which previously existed but goes further where manners and respect for all others involved in the sport are the necessary ingredients for a successful team. The author expects that children will care for and respect their ponies.

To assist coaches the book includes six example lesson plans which between them cover the variety of skills required in mounted games. Clearly David Harris' efforts as a coach are there to win competitions but, above all, throughout his book, he makes it very clear that mounted games must be fun for all involved.

Roger Braham OAM
President 1991—2009
Pony Club Association of NSW

David Harris coached my three daughters in the New South Wales Pony Club state development squad over six years and they have all gone on to represent New South Wales at National Championships, and Australia in the four-nations International Mounted Games Exchange. They have also been very successful in Australian Mounted Games Association national pairs and individual championships.

David is an experienced and insightful coach with many years of experience teaching mounted games at local, state and national level. This book is a testament to David's expertise and the way in which he scrutinises each race and then breaks it down into its different components and skills. By compartmentalising the different skills required, riders are able to improve their riding skills and this allows them to become more competitive at all levels of competition. David's ability to observe then convey those observations into a meaningful guide make this a 'must read' book. It is a great guide for those who are new to mounted games, and for those experienced riders looking for an edge to be able to compete successfully at higher levels.

I would recommend this book to any rider, coach or parent who has an interest in mounted games.

Robyn Slater
Wamboin
New South Wales
Australia

EQUESTRIAN
MOUNTED GAMES

BASIC CONSIDERATIONS FOR
COACHES, INSTRUCTORS AND RIDERS

DAVID HARRIS

FOREWORD BY
HRH THE DUKE OF EDINBURGH

ECHO BOOKS

First published in 2014 by Barrallier Books Pty Ltd, trading as Echo Books

Registered Office: 35-37 Gordon Avenue, West Geelong, Victoria 3220, Australia.

www.echobooks.com.au

National Library of Australia Cataloguing-in-Publication entry (pbk).

Author: Harris, David, 1957- author.

Title: Equestrian Mounted Games : basic considerations for coaches, instructors and riders /David Harris.

ISBN: 9780992444884 (paperback)

Subjects: Equestrian Mounted Games. Games on horseback. Horsemanship--Coaching Horsemanship--Competitions. Horse shows--Rules..

Dewey Number: 798.2

Book and cover design by Peter Gamble, Ink Pot Graphic Design, Canberra.
Set in Garamond Premier Pro 12/17 and Minerva

Back cover photograph by Equiscape Photography

www.echobooks.com.au

CONTENTS

Many people have ideas, but only time and experience can decide whether they will turn out to be good ideas. The origin of what became known as The Pony Club Mounted Games was a casual conversation I had with Colonel Sir Michael Ansell after dinner while staying at Badminton House for the Horse Trials. Sir Michael was a retired cavalry officer and was closely involved in practically every equestrian activity in the country.

The subject of the conversation turned to involvement of children and young people in horse shows. I suggested that the only competitions open to young people were show-jumping events and show classes. I asked Sir Michael whether there was any possibility of involving 'the family children's pony'. He suggested that the 'gymkhana' events, which he had experienced while training for the cavalry, might be an idea. With that the Pony Club Mounted Games came into existence.

I welcome this book by David Harris. The development of any sport depends on the accumulation of knowledge and experience, and I am quite sure that this book will prove to be a great help to future trainers and organisers.

AUTHOR'S ACKNOWLEDGEMENT

I would like to acknowledge the many wonderful people I have had the pleasure of dealing with in the Pony Club Association of New South Wales (PCANSW) of Australia and the Australian Mounted Games Association (AMGA). In particular, from the PCANSW, I would like to acknowledge the outstanding efforts of Rob Bennett, Roger Braham and Phil Logue in establishing the PCANSW elite athlete training squad for mounted games, for introducing me and my family to mounted games, and for their support when I was asked to step into Rob's shoes after family commitments saw him step aside from the PCANSW mounted games squad commitments in 2007. I also acknowledge the support and encouragement I received from the Pony Club Australia when, in 2009 and 2010, my wife Diane and I were selected as the chaperone and coach of the Australian team that participated in the International Mounted Games Exchange between Great Britain, Australia, Canada and the USA.

I learned a great deal from watching and talking to Peter Nelson who is a brilliant saddler and accomplished horseman, Max and Brad French, Sean Corbin and Dan Foster and many others from the AMGA. I would also like to acknowledge and thank my riding instructor, Sally Jones, for her continued support and understanding in helping me train young riders as she helped me transition from a 38 year old ex-footballer to someone who can, with some confidence now, ride and train a horse.

I would also like to thank the riders I have had the pleasure to coach over the years for their trust in me and for putting up with my military communication idiosyncrasies and my old fashioned view of the world.

I would particularly like to thank the wonderful parents of the younger riders I have coached in the PCANSW mounted games elite athlete training squad, for without their amazing support our training sessions could not have been as effective as they were. Their efforts in bringing the riders and ponies to the training venues, marking out fields of play, positioning and endlessly repositioning equipment and even feeding me, keeping me hydrated, and ensuring I was shaded from the Australian sun, significantly enhanced my enjoyment of working with the riders and ponies. These relationships have been particularly rewarding for me and watching their young riders grow into outstanding young adults over time has been both reward in itself and humbling at the same time.

I would very much like to thank Fred von Reibnitz for his persistent encouragement for me to write this book and his assistance in the editing process. Thanks also to Major Michael Tyquin for his advice and subtle prompting, Chris Dyson for his generous support with his camera, skill and time, all the riders who happily assisted me, and to both the AMGA and the PCANSW mounted games coach Anthony Newham, for allowing me to photograph riders during their programmed competitions and training activities.

My thanks also to Jens Martin, the International Development Officer of the International Mounted Games Association (IMGA), for his assistance in helping me tailor this book for IMGA members as well as pony club audiences.

I would very much like to thank Major General Ian Gordon (Retired) and his publishing company, Barrallier Books, for their professional assistance in turning this training manual and its supporting resources for coaches and riders into a reality and the quality product you see today.

I would also like to acknowledge the support of my wife Diane, who was responsible for the final edit of the book, and our daughters Anna and Danielle. Without the understanding and support of all three I could not have committed myself so fully as a coach, and perhaps mentor, to the riders I had the pleasure to coach.

BACKGROUND

1. In 1957 His Royal Highness, Prince Philip, and Colonel Sir Michael Ansell developed and instigated mounted games for Pony Club riders in the United Kingdom with the intent of allowing young riders to compete and enjoy riding where the size, shape and looks of the pony were not important but where the training of the pony and riding skills of the riders were rewarded. Prince Philip Mounted Games were instigated as an equestrian discipline within The Pony Club in the United Kingdom which, over the years, exported the discipline throughout the Pony Club movement internationally.

2. In Australia, for example, Prince Philip has donated a perpetual trophy which is awarded annually at the National Championship to the winning State junior (under 17 years of age) mounted games team. The Pony Club movement in both Canada and the United States of America also embrace this exciting discipline and they also refer to the games as 'Prince Philip Mounted Games'.

3. Prince Philip Mounted Games proved to be so much fun for riders and support personnel that when young riders left the Pony Club movement due to their age, or they passed (in the case of the UK) the eligibility age for participation in Prince Philip Mounted Games, the International Mounted Games Association (IMGA) was formed to cater for the growing demand to continue to play and compete in equestrian mounted games.

4. Equestrian mounted games are now played in Europe, Australia, New Zealand, North America and South Africa with around 10,000 participants. That number is expected to grow as the IMGA committee continues its good work to grow the sport and as Pony Clubs around the world continue to encourage and support young riders to learn and practice this exciting equestrian discipline.

INTRODUCTION

5.   When I was first asked to coach a junior mounted games team some years ago, I had a flashback to the Bill Cosby skit where God talks to Noah about the need for him to build an ark. The skit for those who have not heard it starts with the Lord asking Noah to build him an ark. And Noah says: 'RIGHT! ...What's an ark?'

6.   When I was asked if my daughter could join our pony club's mounted games team when she was about 12 or 13, I said with a flashback to Cosby, 'Sure, ... what's mounted games?' Within 12 months I found myself coaching the club's 'Little Legends' and that started my interest and commitment to both the sport of equestrian mounted games and the amazing people who support and participate in it.

7.   The inspiration for this book grew out of a sense of frustration at there being nowhere to find and absorb knowledge through the experience of others. I could find no reference sources for anyone who had been asked to train a mounted games team and who had no prior exposure to mounted games. Similarly, there is limited reference material for riders who want to enjoy participating in mounted games in either IMGA or AMGA, or through Pony Clubs, but who have no, or limited, exposure to experienced mentors.

8.   In my development as a Pony Club club-level coach[1], and later at the state and national level, I had to rely on watching and listening to several very good mentors and watching and talking to some very talented games riders. They provided me with my understanding of how the games should be played for maximum safe enjoyment of the sport. This book has been written to help mounted games coaches, trainers and riders consider mounted games-related techniques that have been tested and refined over more than 15 years. While techniques are being continually improved by innovative coaches and riders, the pointers raised in this book are not only safe but represent best practice as I perceive it. Other observations I would like to make early in this book are:

---

1   In Australia.

a.   The overall experience of mounted games has to be fun for everyone concerned. I have formed a view that mounted games is most fun when the values expressed and demonstrated by riders and support staff, parents and others are those we typically consider family values.

b.   In Pony Club, mounted games is a team sport[2] and, as such, teamwork is the hallmark of an enjoyable experience for all concerned.

The whole family gets involved.

(1)   Teamwork is based on mutual respect and self-discipline within the team and is best achieved when the team is based on friendship groups where members respect each other's abilities and, yes, frailties.

(2)   I do not believe a team can be fun to be a part of when the team members merely 'tolerate' each other. Effective, enjoyable teamwork comes from respecting each other's strengths and weaknesses. This is most easily seen in the way a team communicates within the team and between team members and support staff, other competitors and indeed with their own ponies[3].

2   In IMGA/AMGA, equestrian mounted games are played as individual and pairs competitions as well as teams competitions.

3   When I take teams to state and national competitions I draw on my formal military leadership training in discussing how we communicate with our words, body language and our deeds. I stress that the reason we all participate in mounted games in our various capacities is because it's fun and, for those of us in support roles, it is rewarding to help others have fun in a safe manner.

Good communication between team members.

PRECONDITIONS

9. For mounted games to be safe and fun for all involved in them, three major
    preconditions need to be satisfied or worked towards to prepare a rider for an
    enjoyable experience:

    a.   the selection of a suitable pony[4],

    b.   good horsemanship and training, and

    c.   mastery of the techniques associated with the actual conduct of the games.

Horse selection

10. The mounted games pony needs to be able to handle fast movement with multiple
    stimuli and remain calm before, during and after the game. While much of this can
    be achieved in time through the use of 'operant conditioning'/training[5], there is a
    sound argument for putting young riders on experienced, older ponies only. Young
    ponies with potential should be trained and ridden in competition by experienced
    riders until they are safe for junior riders to practice and compete on. I have no
    preference for breed or colour when it comes to judging the abilities of a games
    pony. An outstanding games pony is agile, fit and responsive to light commands.
    As I will discuss later, such responsiveness has to be trained and achieved over time.
    While a games pony should be agile and fit, I have also seen some old, slow ponies

---

4   Throughout this book I use 'pony' and 'horse' interchangeably. In Australia most mounted games
    horses tend to be on the smaller side, but horses and ponies of all sizes can be used. As long as they are
    responsive and nimble around the equipment, and the rider can vault on them safely and effectively, size
    is not an issue. IMGA mounts may not exceed 15 hands in competition, but bigger horses can be used
    to play games for the fun of it.

5   A form of repetitive exposure to stimuli and response. I highly recommend that you refer to the work
    of Dr Andrew McLean, an internationally recognized equine behavioural practitioner, especially his
    Academic Horse Training , for more information and insights into horse training techniques.

guiding young riders around; they are safe and I would trust my grandson on them. They are fantastic ponies for beginners, even if they would not win a 'Prettiest Pony' class at the local agricultural show.

11. I do get concerned when I see young riders on strong, very fast ponies that are not responsive to riding commands. I become even more concerned when I see such a pony in the hands of a rider who does not have the knowledge or experience to give the right commands at the right time, to recognise the pony's attempt to respond to the command or to reward the correct response (or a reasonable attempt) when they do get it from the pony.

12. My advice in horse selection is to opt for the safe pony and work on its agility and responsiveness. When the rider has the bilateral coordination[6], reflexes, skill and knowledge to train a pony, then the younger, more agile and faster pony can be selected. Do not expect such a pony to be perfect soon. It can take up to two years of moderate work for the pony to understand its task and to give the rider some clean fast runs while remaining calm itself.

13. What do I like to see in a prospective games pony while in-hand? I like a pony to allow me to touch it all over without flinching or tossing its head to get my hand off it. I like to see a pony that is happy to lift any hoof when asked by light pressure on its tendon. I especially like to see a pony that backs up to light pressure from the rein or lead rope and I like a pony that stands and does not fidget. I also like a pony that moves its hindquarters with an adductive movement of its hind leg[7] when I apply light pressure back from the girth—similar to the aid given to leg yield.

14. What do I like to see in a prospective games pony under saddle? I like to see a pony that:

    a.   stands still while the rider mounts[8],

    b.   will turn its head to single rein pressure and not move off (unless leg pressure is applied),

---

6   Able to give aids to the horse independently through either hand, either leg and/or seat and body position.

7   Where the inside hind leg/hoof is placed in front of or past the outside hind hoof as it moves its hindquarters away from the gentle pressure behind the girth. It is instructive to do this on both sides as it provides an indication of the responsiveness of the pony to leg yield commands and canter lead aids.

8   Though some riders when learning to mount can make the pony unbalanced or even accidentally ask the pony to move with unintended rein or leg aids.

  c. moves off/goes forward to light but even pressure of the lower legs,

  d. stops from light seat and rein pressure and/or voice command,

  e. listens to its rider (you can see the ears rotate back when you talk to them with a voice command to reinforce a leg, seat or rein command—my oldest daughter would sometimes sing to her pony before and after a race and it appeared to calm them both),

  f. backs up easily with light pressure as this is insurance for the stop command,

  g. moves in either direction to single rein pressure—the inside rein open or the outside rein closed on the neck,

  h. is not fazed by coloured equipment or other ponies moving in its close vicinity (i.e. in handover situations), and

  i. responds to leg yielding aids at walk, trot and canter and is able to drift left or right at the canter or gallop from lower leg pressure on the girth.

15. As you can see, I am looking for a pony well-schooled in the fundamentals of dressage, that is not fazed by coloured equipment or other ponies close by, and can transition down from a gallop to immobility for the rider to execute a handover and walk back to the team on a loose rein ready to commence the next race.

16. Such ponies are not easy to find. In fact most people will often not sell such a pony. Good games ponies are made through considerate, deliberate training that is graduated to reflect the learning abilities of the pony or horse. Indeed I own one and it took years of dressage and games training by my oldest daughter for him to be the legend that is 'Jasper'. He is not the best looking pony in the world by a long way, but he will be just what my grandson will need if he chooses to participate in mounted games in the future.

Horsemanship

17. A mounted games pony should be treated with respect and its welfare held paramount during its use in mounted games. Riders must take the time to train it to do its many tasks calmly and on command. I prefer light, well understood commands that have come through considered and considerate training, as compared to heavy-handed, painful commands.

18. The role of the coach is important in ensuring that riders are balanced in their upright seat, three point seat and two point seat, and are able to give clear commands to their mount. The riding skills required of a good mounted games rider are:

a. ride a straight line in walk, trot and canter;

b. ride a straight line while transitioning up and down through the gaits;

c. ride a circle on the left or right rein where the pony is flexed to the inside and the hind hooves fall in the tracks of the front hooves;

d. control the pony's shoulders by achieving soft and compliant nearside and offside flexion[9];

e. stop the pony in three beats of its footfall from all three gaits;

f. back the pony up with soft pressure;

g. leg yield left and right; and

h. be able to achieve the offside and nearside canter lead on command

The two point seat employed in the hoon zone.

19. As can be seen from this list, a games rider needs to train their pony with basic dressage. Given that dressage was invented to train a knight's steed or a cavalryman's charger to take their riders into battle, where controlling the horse with limited rein contact (the rider having to wield his weapons) was the norm, it makes eminent sense for dressage to form the basis for all mounted games riding.

20. Horsemanship also implies the rider's care for their mount. Riders should be strongly encouraged to feed, water and groom their own pony and ensure its

---

9   Flexion exercises become very important to allow the rider to get close to equipment, by flexing the pony's head away from the equipment but still guiding its shoulders into the vicinity of the equipment. A pony that focuses on the equipment, especially if it has some concern about approaching it, may bring its head close to the equipment but swing its hindquarters out, taking the rider beyond the reach of the equipment and the task that needs to be undertaken. The rider needs to be careful, however, that the neck is not overly bent when the pony flexes at the poll, as this may make control of the pony's shoulders more difficult to maintain.

comfort when travelling or stabled. Hoof care is particularly important. A lame pony should not be ridden and, apart from the horse welfare issues, it is a shame if a rider's good work cannot be seen because of a lack of attention to the pony's hooves.

Training the mounted games pony

21. **Trained to respond to soft commands.** The games pony should be trained to give a single response from a single command[10]. That training starts slowly with ground work (in-hand) by teaching the pony to 'park'[11], move forward off light pressure and to stop and back-up to light pressure. Coaches need to train their riders to give their pony precautionary warning so that the pony becomes attentive and light to commands. In mounted games, voice commands make excellent precautionary warnings for the pony, as does the half halt[12] when the pony is being ridden. These precautionary warnings are given one or two beats before the actual command to change gait, stop, or stand.

22. **Equipment considerations for an animal wired for flight.** Horses are instinctively cautious and are prepared to flee from unusual or potentially threatening situations. When preparing a pony to play mounted games it is important to understand this instinctive reaction to unfamiliar events, and to introduce ponies to new stimuli slowly and to gradually decrease the proximity (how close the pony can get to the equipment without it getting scared or worried). Very few ponies are able to ignore or disregard the presence of colourful, noisy or flapping equipment without first being desensitised to it. During breaking, the breaker should have 'bagged the horse down' to make it comfortable around whips cracking in its vicinity, bags and rugs being used around and on the horse, and these actions are familiarised with the horse on both sides. Most ponies, however, are not introduced to mounted games equipment when they are broken in, so it is necessary to introduce the games pony to new equipment slowly and considerately.

---

10   Such as 'go, stop, stand, change gait, take the correct lead, flex, increase or decrease length of stride, move the shoulders, yield'.

11   See paragraph 28 for an explanation of 'parking'.

12   In the half halt the rider momentarily and deliberately puts greater pressure on the outside seat bone while keeping their seat in the same rhythm as the horse; this can be accompanied by light rein or outside rein pressure. Once the horse gets used to the precautionary warning it will await the next command and this allows softer commands to be given.

23. **Mica's story.** Mica is a wonderful young palomino mare my wife bred. She stands
     at 14.2 hands high and carries a mixture of Arabian, warmblood, thoroughbred,
     stockhorse and Quarter Horse blood. I have been preparing her for potential use by
     my grandchildren if they want to ride when they are old enough. Consequently we
     have been confirming the basics in dressage and jumping lessons and general riding.
     When I decided that she should also be an accomplished games pony I found that
     she was flighty around the equipment even though she had been very well broken
     in. The solution with Mica was simple: we took her back to basics from the ground/
     in-hand and familiarised her with the equipment for each game for which we were
     training her. Let's consider how we familiarised her with the Litter / Litter Lifters
     Race.[13]

     a. I used the stick to pick up and rattle (gently at first) the litter on the stick
         on the nearside, and her immediate reaction was to pull back. Expecting this
         reaction, I kept the litter on the stick, rattling gently, and moved back with
         her indicating that her flight response would not be rewarded with me taking
         the gently rattling equipment away.

     b. Even though she was clearly uneasy with this introduction I used a gentle
         voice to reassure her that it was not a 'horse eating' piece of litter, and she
         eventually stood for me while I was able to move the litter on a stick so it
         touched her. Then I touched her gently with it over her body—just like when
         she was bagged when she was broken in.

     c. I then went through the same procedure on the offside.

     d. With her still in-hand, I then started picking the litter up and flicking it up and
         forward and, later, sideways as well. I started with small movements first and
         increased them as she permitted. Again her immediate reaction was to retreat
         but, again, a gentle voice and quiet persistence saw her accept this sometimes
         stationary and sometimes flying piece of litter. Again, I did this also on the offside.

     e. I then mounted and, from a standing/stationary position, just pushed the litter
         around with the stick, similar to what I had done in-hand. It was important
         to keep her calm with my voice, touch and minimal movement in the saddle.
         (At this point a coach could help a young rider by holding the pony and
         encouraging it to stand still if the rider has difficulty.)

---

13   Where the same or similar race is conducted within both Pony Club and IMGA, I have provided both
     versions of the race name in this book, Pony Club first and IMGA version second.

f. I then set up the litter on a barrel so that I would not have to lean down to pick up the litter (thereby ensuring that I did not introduce two new stimuli at once—the litter and my changed body weight as I reached down to pick it up).

g. We then proceeded to pick up and put down the litter on the drum and she handled it like a veteran.

h. I then tried the same action but with the litter sitting on a milk crate, which required me to lean down a little to pick up the equipment. (The new stimulus this time was my slight weight movement while picking up the now boring piece of litter.)

i. We then moved rapidly to picking the litter up from the standing position, which was now easy for her.

j. Lastly we tried it on the move, and she had a mild 'brain snap', and darted forward as soon as I was momentarily out of contact with the saddle. These things happen—I had probably been too hasty.

k. So we went back to the standing pick-up and then ever so slowly introduced a little movement and stop into the drill.

l. Within five minutes she was happily picking up the litter from the walk, and that was definitely enough for her litter race lesson for the day.

Note 1. At the next games training session I had with Mica it was important to go back a few steps to 'remind' her what she had learned by me touching the litter and pushing it around on the ground in front of her while mounted before attempting to pick it up stationary and then on the move at the walk.

Note 2. Training is one thing and competition is another. When I next competed on her she was fine with the approach to and standing at the litter/equipment, until the neighbouring horse's hooves thundered up next to us. She lost focus on the job at hand and wanted to 'get out of there'. We then had to persist, so I relied on 'back-up' commands to settle her and then I pushed the litter around a few times—reminding her that 'hey, this is not actually scary'—then I was able to pick it up. I can assure you it was not pretty, but the other team members were very understanding and supportive of my need to continue the mare's training. The lesson is that it takes time, consideration and persistence to train your horse from scratch, and the competition environment is an important part of the training process.

Note 3. In subsequent competitions I increased the pace for us both and found the next issue: the litter rattled loudly on the stick during windy conditions. It was no surprise to me but Mica reacted as if she had just heard a rhinoceros charging towards her rear end. I did the best we could on the day but the following Saturday it was back to the quiet training on the ground next to her, holding the stick and rattling the litter on it under her neck, above her ears and near her rump on both sides until she was absolutely bored with it. I don't blame her for her reaction to the new combination of stimuli, as we had increased the speed and ridden in other than fair weather conditions. It just shows that she has a brain, will think for herself and that the training was not as thorough as it should have been.

Note 4. After several competitions Mica has become better and better at this and other games. The lesson here is that for a horse to be good at competition you have to continue its training during competitions and be prepared to fix issues using the same original techniques. A supportive and understanding team environment is most helpful when training the new games pony.

24. **Lessons from Mica's story.** Mica had been broken in as a three year old and 'learned how to learn' from pressure and pressure release techniques. My breaker would apply an aid, and then keep it applied until she gave a response that resembled the required response. As soon as that response was achieved the pressure was relieved and she was told in a gentle voice what a clever horse she was, sometimes she would also be stroked gently on the neck, and she was allowed to think about that for a while. Then the same stimulus (aid) was applied again and he would wait until a reasonable effort was achieved in the direction of the response required and immediately relieve the pressure again, and use a gentle voice and soft pat to reinforce the response she gave. Over time Mica learned that when pressure was applied a response was required, and if she was not sure what response was required she would try several things. Then, when she got it about right, the pressure was withdrawn and the desired behaviour was reinforced with a gentle voice and sometimes a soft pat. The technique I used to train her for the Litter Race, as described above, mirrored exactly the techniques my breaker had used when he broke her in. Take it slowly at first—don't relieve pressure until the desired response, or something like it in the early days, is achieved or attempted, and reward the desired responses by immediately relieving the pressure

25. **Andrew McLean's drawing pin example.** At this point it seems appropriate to relate a story Dr Andrew McLean told a group at one of his clinics that my wife and I attended. Dr McLean described a practical joke scenario from his school days where it was seen as funny to induce a flight response in someone by sticking

a drawing pin to their seat with the point uppermost, and watching the response when the unsuspecting victim sat on the pin. Unsurprisingly the victim would jump up quickly.

26. Dr McLean asked us all why the victim had jumped up and the response from the audience was: 'Because it hurt'. Dr McLean's response, however, has stuck with me since. He said: 'Not quite, the victim jumped up quickly to be relieved from the pain'. He then brought this analogy to how he recommends that horses be trained: provide an irritation (through the bit, legs or seat) and then stop the irritating behaviour as soon as the desired response is achieved. When coupled with a precautionary action or voice signal, the horse learns to expect to change its movement or rhythm and is able to respond gently and quietly without the need to inflict discomfort/pain by the bit or whip.

27. **Overshadowing.** Overshadowing is a training technique which Dr McLean uses to educate or re-educate horses. The technique relies on the horse being well trained in-hand in the first instance. If the horse he is working with does not have 'good manners' in-hand then the first step is to retrain this behaviour. Again, pressure and pressure release are used to correct a horse's behaviour in-hand. The desired behaviours are that the horse gives the rider space and does not push on the rider. Also, we want the horse to move as a result of pressure, stop in a maximum of three paces as a result of pressure, and then not to move until pressure is applied, usually with the halter or the reins and bit, if the horse is bridled. If a horse does not move to gentle pressure from the halter, a dressage whip is tapped continually but not vigorously on the side of the horse where the lower leg would hang. Once the horse moves off to both the halter pressure and whip tap the latter can be removed altogether.

28. Dr McLean then confirms that the horse can be 'parked'. This is where the horse will stand and let the rider move away from it without following and will stand until the rider returns. It only moves from the parked position when pressure (preferably light pressure) is applied. Dr McLean uses a dressage whip to assist in this training and just taps an errant foreleg that is about to be lifted from the ground in the horse's attempt to follow its rider when the rider moves away. He starts with achieving a small separation distance from both sides of the horse and gradually moves out to greater distances.

29. Once the horse is well mannered in-hand the coach can assist a rider with overshadowing techniques. For example, in Mica's story, if I'd had difficulty with her standing while I leaned over to pick up the litter I could have asked an assistant to take hold of her reins just below the bit, and as she moved in response to my shifting body weight the dressage whip would be employed to tap the 'naughty hoof' that moved when I had not used lower leg pressure (the 'go' button) to ask her to move—just like the parking training the horse received in-hand. Overshadowing can also take the form of transitions, stopping, backing-up, anything that effectively takes the horse's mind off the new 'scary' stimulus and allows it to react to a stimulus that it has been comfortably drilled in. Over time the new stimulus becomes the norm and the horse realises it does not need to flee.

30. Coaches therefore should be prepared to assist new games mounts using 'overshadowing' training techniques if a games pony is reluctant to get close to equipment or stand or let other ponies get close.[14]

31. Riders do get frustrated when their pony gets confused and is not sure what response is required from a given command. It is counterproductive for a rider to get angry with their pony. Of course there are times when we need to be firm, but on such occasions we need to be absolutely consistent and persevere with the command until the correct response (or something resembling it) is achieved. It is then very important to shed the frustration instantly and reward the pony, by voice and soft touch, for getting it right or giving a response that is on the way to getting it right.

Use of spurs in training the games mount

32. There are very good reasons why spurs are not permitted during a mounted games competition. The use of spurs to reinforce the leg aid requires a stable and controlled lower leg. The use of the spur needs to be timed to the instant and the response graduated in terms of angle and pressure. In any game it is possible that a rider will have to mount or dismount quickly and it is often possible for a rider to be temporarily unbalanced and rely on the pony to run straight with the rider's centre of gravity not directly above the pony's spine. On such occasions it is possible to envisage a rider touching a pony with their spurs in areas where the pony has not been trained to expect that pressure, and for that surprising

---

14   See Dr Andrew McLean's excellent books and videos for specific instructions on 'overshadowing' and equestrian training in general.

use of the spur to cause the pony to react spontaneously in an unpredictable or dangerous manner. If riders cannot use spurs in competition it may be counterproductive to train the pony with spurs as, if the training is not perfect, they may only respond to the spur. I do not recommend training the mounted games pony or horse with spurs.

Mastery of the techniques

33. The physical conduct of the games relies on riders developing, practicing and mastering the techniques for handling the equipment so that their actions become instinctive and they execute the correct techniques with accuracy and a light touch, while still giving the pony a balanced ride.

34. Mastery of games techniques does not come easily. It is important to train both the pony and the rider's actions slowly at first to develop the 'muscle memory' required to achieve instinctively soft hands. Similarly, mastering the alternate application of lower leg pressure during a simple bending race to drift the pony between the poles, rather than have the pony curve its spine and therefore take a longer, slower path, takes time, patience and consideration.

35. Training sessions should not be conducted fast all the time. In the early days of a pony/rider combination's training, more time should be spent introducing the pony to the equipment (in-hand initially if required), and practicing the races at the three gaits of walk, trot and canter. It is important that the pony does not practice the same game at the same gait so much that it starts to anticipate the line and pace. Rather, it should be accustomed to employing different gaits for the same race, and perhaps mixing it up so that there are several gaits in each run. When coaching a young team I like to have most of my training sessions slower rather than faster. Getting ready for competition is different, but I would only have about 10-20% of the session at competition speed; the rest of the session is slower than that so that the ponies and riders can concentrate on the tactics and finer points of each game.

Reins

36. Young or inexperienced riders have a tendency, when they are concentrating on the game, to hold the equipment in one hand and steer their pony with a one-handed grip on the reins for the entire race. I believe that the rider has better control for longer if they keep hold of both reins with both hands for as long as is practicable during a game. This

may involve holding a cane, ball, sock or other equipment in the thumb and forefinger of the master hand while the third, fourth and little fingers of that hand keep tension on the rein to give the pony the knowledge that both reins are in play as stop and steering aids. When a one-handed grip on the reins is required I use and recommend the 'stockman's / cavalry grip'. The benefits of this grip are many: it allows single and multiple rein pressure and pressure release, allows for opening rein contact and enables rapid re-collection of a contact if the contact is lost for whatever reason. While it may be difficult for young riders to achieve, it is worth persevering to master the technique.

Use of the 'stockman's grip'.

37. As shown in the photo sequence, the reins are held in the left hand with the offside (right) rein between the index finger and the middle finger, and the nearside (left) rein between the little finger and the ring finger. The loop of the reins is crossed in the palm of the hand with the thumb clamping both reins from behind to stop the reins from being inadvertently lengthened. The nearside rein is able to be opened by slightly relaxing the grip on the index and middle fingers, gripping the nearside rein with the little and ring fingers. Moving the left arm away from the pony's neck puts pressure on the nearside of the pony's mouth while maintaining offside rein pressure on the neck. Reins can be regathered at the buckle with the right hand, when able, and vice versa for opening the offside rein.

Riding seat

38. Riders who use body weight as an aid to steering may be successful on their own pony, but they will have difficulty competing at the highest levels[15] where borrowed ponies are often used. They will also find that as they get older and heavier the number of

---

15   In Australia it is very expensive to compete overseas or even interstate because of transport costs and borrowed ponies are a part of higher training regimes.

ponies that can accommodate such crude commands is limited. The seat positions used in mounted games vary depending on the skills of the rider and mount. Classic riding positions should be employed through the transitions between gaits.

39. **The upright seat.** The upright seat position[16] should be used for those parts of a game where control is required to prepare the pony for a manoeuvre that requires exact lines and an attentive pony. For example handovers (pass-offs), picking up a coin from a coin box, or putting down a ball on a cone. The upright seat is typically used in what I refer to as the 'control zone'.[17]

The upright seat.

40. **The two point seat.** The two point seat[18] is used with even pressure on each side of the saddle from stable lower legs where it is important for the pony to move freely. Typically this is seen in the first half of a Five Flag/Flag Fliers Race or the Litter/Litter Lifters Race. The two point seat is frequently used in what riders often refer to as the 'hoon zones'[19] of a race. It allows the pony

---

16 The rider sits upright to achieve vertical alignment of the heel, hip, shoulder and ear (heels are to be lower than the ball of the foot in the stirrup iron).

17 The control zone is that part of the arena before and just past a piece of equipment where the rider needs to slow the pony to increase their chances of picking up, putting down or handing over equipment, or dismounting under control. The length of the control zone is entirely dependent on the education of the pony and the rider's riding skill and mastery of equipment techniques.

18 The rider stands forward of the upright position, clear of the saddle with a straight back to achieve a straight line through toe, knee and shoulder (again, the heels must be lower than the toes in the stirrup irons).

19 The 'hoon zone' is an Australian term used to describe that part of a race where the rider can let the pony run freely.

to run freely with the rider balanced, with minimum pressure on the pony's mouth.

The two point seat.

41.   **The three point seat.** The three point seat[20] is typically used in mounted games when transitioning down from the two point seat as the rider approaches a control zone. Depending on the control required, the three point seat may be a precursor to the upright seated position in the control zone, i.e. handovers (pass-offs). The rider's legs and seat are in contact with the saddle and the rider's rhythm is quickly synchronised with the pony for greater control.

The three point seat.

---

20   Rider sits forward of the upright position in the same line as two point, but the third point of contact on the saddle is the seat.

42. It is recommended that coaches reinforce with riders the need for a balanced ride as lines of approach will be more efficient, and the ponies will stay fresher longer because the rider will make fewer mistakes.

SAFETY

43. Equestrian mounted games are potentially dangerous if standard controls are not applied. The successful training of the mounted games pony is the fundamental aid to achieving safety in mounted games. The rules for individual games and the penalties for violating those rules are often designed to keep the rider safe. Riders therefore, need to be aware of the rules and understand why they are important for their safety. Other standard safety controls that need to be applied for every training session or competition activity include the correct layout of the playing field, safe/disciplined handover or pass-off techniques and safe vaulting techniques. The following safety suggestions are recommended.

Playing field

44. The following conditions apply in competition and should be considered where applicable in training situations. Detailed guidance should, however, be sought from your Pony Club or Mounted Games Association handbooks prior to competitions. The playing area of a games arena is usually 60m long, with 6m long changeover boxes behind the start/finish line and behind the changeover line at the far end of the playing area.

45. **An arena of sufficient size.** The minimum recommended in the Club or Association guidance is advantageous. It should:

   a. offer an enclosed/bounded arena (bunting may be used as a temporary enclosure for training or championships held outdoors) and where possible be:

     (1) free of obstructions and slip/trip hazards, and

     (2) free of rocks and trees;

   b. offer flat to gently undulating terrain if held outdoors;

c. accommodate lane widths sufficient for the competence of the teams/riders participating (I prefer at least 10m between lanes of equipment when training young riders);

d. allow for a run-off area for emergency use and ensure that all riders are briefed in its use (I brief all riders that they are to turn right into run-off areas);

e. offer sufficient space to accommodate marshalling areas, and spectator and warm-up areas;

f. allow equipment to be placed close to where it will be needed during the training activity or competition, but out of the way—this may need to be bunted off from spectators and riders;

g. accommodate line stewards located in the lanes or to the side of the arena; and

h. accommodate the starter in line with the first line of bending poles with consideration given to providing them with a slightly elevated stable platform from which they can see the start line for all lanes.

Arena layout incorporates safety spaces, coloured lines for colour-blind riders, and equipment prepared for easy lane allocation

46. **Safety space.** The aim of a safety space is to create a gap or space between your team and any other riders/teams so that if a pony loses its rider in the field of play it has a space through which to run as it thunders back to its mates, rather than having no option but to run into strung-out ponies. Other safety space considerations include:

a. **Entering the arena.** A team entering an arena for competition or training should be in a line abreast formation with the riders almost touching stirrup to stirrup. Any pony still undergoing training and not completely comfortable in the close company of other ponies should be on the outside of the formation.

b. **Team in the 'ready' position.** The team should adopt the 'ready' position in their allocated lane upon entering the arena in a competition or in preparation for the start of a race when training. It is the signal to the coach/starter that the team is ready to commence the next race. The ready position allows:

(1) at least 10m (more if possible) back from the start line;

(2) four ponies and riders facing up the arena[21], stirrup to stirrup if the ponies will allow, in the order they will compete in during the race;

(3) if bunting is used to define the playing field, the team should stand at least 2m off the bunting to give room for a loose pony to pass unhindered behind the team; if an arena wall defines the playing field, riders should also leave room behind them for an errant pony to pass unhindered behind them; and

(4) a safety space either side of the team, usually of several metres.

The 'ready' position, with safety space between teams.

---

21 When racing, the riders are lined up, facing up the arena, right to left in the order in which they will play the game. The rider on the right of the line is the first to leave; the rider on the left of the line is the last to leave and in a competition will wear an identifying cap cover, arm band or other identifying mark to assist judges to award placings correctly.

47. **Handover (pass-off) technique.** Handovers should always be right hand to right hand. Here are hints that may be useful in executing safe handover drills:

   a. **Outgoing rider advances as incoming rider transitions down.** Handovers are much safer if the incoming rider is transitioning down in speed and gait as the outgoing rider is moving forward (but is definitely not stationary[22]).

   b. **Rider's position in handover box.** The rider's position in the handover box should normally be dictated by the outgoing rider's need for the optimal line with which to commence their game. Therefore the incoming rider has a responsibility to adjust their line to allow the outgoing rider to set themselves early. However, the outgoing rider should also be prepared to adjust to the needs of the incoming rider as it does not always transpire that the incoming rider has sufficient time to adjust their line. In those circumstances it is the responsibility of the outgoing rider to avert an accident in the changeover box and leg yield their pony to the best/safest position to effect the handover or, if necessary, 'bail-out' of the handover completely and thereby ensure that both riders and ponies are fit for the next race.

   c. **The arm in the handover.** The position of the arm for both giving and receiving equipment during the handover is important. The arm needs to be forward of the body on an angle of 45 degrees to the front, with a bent elbow (the arm should not be stretched out), fingers of the receiving/outgoing rider need to be spread wide to offer a viable target into which the incoming rider places the equipment. The incoming rider may be riding in a two point seat in preparation for the handover but should transition down to three point as their left hand takes the reins in the single-handed grip and prepares to move to apply slight right rein pressure with the left hand[23]. Both riders have to align their hands in height so that the equipment can be transferred smoothly. This can be problematic if a small pony/rider combination is in the team or if there is a large horse with a small rider. In this case the coach needs to pick the best combinations for the handover and practice that. The outgoing rider has a responsibility to take the equipment being offered.

---

22   Over the years I have seen several very well trained ponies injured during a handover that went wrong because the pony did as it was told and stood still waiting for a go command from a rider who was fixated on the incoming rider and did not move the pony away from a bad line ridden by the incoming rider. A moving pony is more likely to take evasive action on its own initiative if moving forward—albeit at the walk.

23   This achieves a turn and halt on the right rein while the right hand is critically in play with the handover. See also sub-paragraph 49.c. (and footnote 30) which explains the right hand turn using the left hand

Arm position forward of the body and angled to the front.

d.   **Cushion the handover.** Control by the incoming rider is critical to effecting a safe handover[24]. The coach's catch cry during handover training is often: 'Cushion the handover, watch the equipment ('Look Back')'. The cushioned handover is a strategy that requires both the incoming and the outgoing riders to hand over/take the equipment in a rearwards motion of the arm while the pony moves forward, with emphasis on looking back to ensure that the handover is observed by both riders[25] At the point of handover I like to see a gap of about 40cm between opposing knees but I acknowledge that this is sometimes too ambitious for very young riders with short arms. The incoming rider should continue the downwards transition by reverting to the upright seated position and finish the handover by turning the pony on the right rein and/or halting[26] and stopping it close to the point of handover. This does not have to be done slowly and it positions the incoming rider very close to the most likely drop point for a quick recovery if the equipment is fumbled and dropped. The soft handover at speed is achieved with cushioning effect by both riders handing the equipment backwards as they move forwards through the handover. The twist of the shoulders (looking back) gives an extra half metre

---

24   Depending on the horse and rider combination, it might be prudent to train the riders to adopt the upright seat immediately before the right turn/cushion (look-back) in the handover. Horses and coaches do not appreciate the rider being unbalanced and forward when they turn quickly in a handover.

25   I acknowledge that some elite-level IMGA teams disagree with this drill of looking back in a handover. While I can see their arguments for the practice of outgoing riders looking to their next task, on balance I prefer the cushioned handover with both riders watching the equipment at that critical point in time.

26   With the left hand.

extension/cushion by each rider. This technique is used as confidence and speed of handovers increases.

Cushioned/soft handover.

e.   **'Hunt out' the next rider.** The transition down and turn to halt manoeuvre executed by the incoming rider just behind the point of handover has the added benefit of encouraging a young, or less willing, outgoing mount to leave the handover box.

Hunting out the next pony.

f.   **Stop, stand and reward the horse.** Once the outgoing rider has safely left the handover box and has entered the field of play, the incoming rider should insist that their pony stop all forward momentum and stop/stand[27]

---

27   Known as 'immobility' in dressage tests.

in the box, facing up the field of play so that the rider maintains their situational awareness of the game. I like the rider to give the pony a pat (gentling motion) low on the neck near the withers and, with a loose rein, move off to the left of the line of the rest of the team. This must be practiced so that in competition the ponies become calm immediately after their run and are therefore calm for the whole day.

Pony stands calmly in preparation for next task.

g.   **The walk back.** The walk back to the rest of the team should be on the left rein to avoid moving in front of the next rider to move off, and the rider positions their pony to the outside of the team (to the left of the line).

Pony walks back on the left rein.

h.   **Make room.** The rest of the team leg-yields right 1.5m or so to accommodate the latest rider forming back up in a safe knot of riders but still in their allocated lane, while maintaining their safety space on either side of the team and their orientation looking up the field of play.

Team leg yields to right to allow rider and pony to rejoin the line.

48.   **When to abort or 'bail out' of a handover.** I tell my riders it is a joint responsibility to conduct handovers safely. If either rider feels a handover line, pony orientation or speed does not feel right they are to abort or bail out of the handover. The bail-out drill is where one or both riders move away from the handover using the left rein to separate ponies and riders at the final stages of the approach. Often a bail-out will be executed because an outgoing rider has lost control of their pony's hindquarters and they have swung them into the path of the incoming pony or, conversely, it might be that the outgoing pony's head has moved into the path of the incoming rider, thereby eliminating any safety space between riders. Outgoing rider control issues can usually be fixed by timing the move forward and keeping the pony moving straight rather than having to check the pony in the changeover box because it was brought up too soon[28]. Incoming rider issues often arise when the rider does not have sufficient control to adjust the speed or line of the pony. In such cases

---

28   I know that rules for handovers in Pony Club competitions in the UK in 2010 stipulated that the outgoing rider must come into the changeover box and be stationary before moving into the handover. I disagree with this risk control strategy as I feel it would be better to insist on the incoming rider stopping in the changeover box, thereby forcing a deceleration at the point of most likely accidents.

the outgoing rider should definitely bailout of the handover to ensure they stay fit and well to try again next race, rather than risk a collision which is not good for riders, ponies or the sport in general.

Either rider, or both, can bailout to the left if they feel it's unsafe.

Incoming rider considerations

49. Ideally, the incoming rider needs to have an understanding of where the next rider will be in the changeover box and ride a line that gives the outgoing rider priority in the box. Additional hints for incoming riders are:

   a. **Riding positions.** Often the incoming rider will be using a two point seat as close as 15m from the point of handover. In the intervening distance the rider drops their seat to the three point seat and synchronises their seat in the saddle with the rhythm of the pony, at the same time ensuring that the lower leg position has not moved from the two point position. After the first two or three synchronised strides with the pony the rider adjusts the reins to allow for a controlled one-handed right turn and, as the point of handover approaches, the rider leans slightly back into the upright seat while still synchronising their movements to that of the pony (this means that there should not be daylight between the rider's seat and the saddle as they transition down to the handover). As the handover is effected, the incoming rider should continue to stay deep in the saddle and turn and stop the pony to face back up the arena. Note that exuberant riders who reach forward to offer the handover take their seat out of the saddle and stop riding the pony into the downwards transition. In reaching forward they also tend to lean forward with their toes pointing to the ground, and the likelihood of becoming unseated is increased.

b.   **Control.** The incoming rider must have their pony under control to achieve a safe handover. If the rider feels that the pony is pulling too strongly or is not responding, the rider must not try to effect the handover by taking one hand off the reins. Best control of a pony is achieved with even pressure on the reins. Both riders are responsible for the safe handover/conduct of the game and if either rider feels the handover has potential to hurt either riders or ponies they must abort the handover and yield their pony away from potential danger[29]. In the pictures below the incoming rider misjudged the line and the great little pony with the young rider sidestepped on his own initiative.

A good pony looks after its rider!

c.   **Hold and offer the equipment**. The equipment is held and offered so that it can be taken by the outgoing rider with minimum adjustment in their hand to be able to do their first task with the equipment. For example, in the Five Flag/Flag Fliers race, the incoming rider should offer the flag/ cane by holding it close to the flag. It MUST be vertical, which allows the outgoing rider to grasp the cane where they like so that they do not have to adjust their grip to place the flag in the cone after exploiting their hoon zone.

d.   **Fingertip grip on equipment.** No matter what the equipment, the incoming rider should offer it with a fingertip grip. The fingertip grip on the equipment

---

29   This is most often to the left, but both riders need to be aware of unfolding events and react in a way that keeps a safety space around themselves if need be.

is secure while not being so strong that the outgoing rider cannot grasp it and pull it out of the incoming rider's grip if necessary. This is particularly useful with tennis balls and socks. This allows the outgoing rider to take the equipment from the incoming rider's grip even if at the last moment the incoming rider has tensed up as a result of excitement or an unexpected pony movement.

The fingertip grip.

e. **One handed transition down, turn and stop during cushion.** The very nature of a handover means that the rider has to control their pony with one hand during the handover. This manoeuvre is made more complex as better teams will strive to both maintain momentum during the handover and position the incoming rider to be able to recover quickly if the equipment is accidentally dropped. If a hoon zone precedes the handover the rider will have to transition down from their two point seat to a three point seat then an upright seat to effect the handover. The reins should be transferred to the left hand after the three point seat has been achieved and the rider is preparing for the upright seat and further transition down. The reins should be held one-handed with the left hand such that the rider can exert pressure on the right rein (with an extended index finger on the right rein usually) to effect a right turn[30] as the handover is being effected, and the rider should look back to confirm that the outgoing rider has the equipment.

---

30 The right turn aid is further supported by the movement of the incoming rider's hips as they cushion the handover and look back to confirm the handover's success.

f. **Prepare for recovery if equipment dropped.** If the equipment is fumbled and dropped in or behind the handover box the incoming rider who has cushioned the handover and turned their pony, and has trained it to stop and face up the lane, is best placed to dismount—usually the offside dismount is quickest in such cases—and retrieve the equipment and pass it from the ground (hand to hand) to the outgoing rider.

Quick recovery—noting that an offside dismount might be advisable depending on location of dropped equipment.

g. **Settle the pony.** After the outgoing pony has left the changeover box it is important to train the incoming pony to settle quickly for the next task. Ensure that the pony stops and stands, albeit momentarily, before rewarding his efforts.

h. **Acknowledge good performance**. Once stationary, pat the pony gently on the lower neck near the withers to emphasise positive feedback, and support this with a gentle/reassuring voice aid.

i. **Walk the pony back to the rest of the team.** If possible, using a long rein, turn the pony to the left and walk the pony back to the left of the team line[31]. Upon joining the line, refocus on the game and be prepared to offer instructions to the rider in play as a 'designated caller', as the rider in play often has a limited view of the game unfolding around them.

50. **Do not ... Do not** ride into the handover with the arm fully stretched either to the front (hand near the pony's ear) or to the side (90 degrees from the line of movement). Of these the former is by far the more dangerous as it brings the riders much too close for comfort; the latter limits the cushion effect (increasing the potential for injury) and gives no flexibility for the rider to chase the handover if one or both ponies move away from the handover at the last instant.

Avoid straight arms in handovers!

Note: When training a team with this technique it is very important that the last rider is offered a handover and is required to practice/train their pony in the handover drill and recovery dismounts. A pony that always runs last may not be practised in the cushion, stop and turn technique and will only be reliable in a number four position, which decreases the team's flexibility if an injury occurs to one of the other riders or their pony.

---

31 By walking back to the team on the left rein the chances of walking the pony in front of the next outgoing rider are lowered.

Outgoing rider considerations

51. As mentioned in paragraph 49, the incoming rider needs to have an understanding of where the next rider will be in the changeover box and ride a line that gives the outgoing rider priority in the box. Additional hints for outgoing riders are:

a. **Position the pony for the start.** Position the pony to the rear of the changeover box so that it adopts the best line for the first part of the race.

b. **Time the advance for the handover.** With the pony under control, time the move forward so that the pony remains straight and forward at walk or trot, head and hindquarters parallel to the lane so that both riders meet about 2m back from the start/finish line.[32]

Outstanding timing in the handover.

c. **Keep the pony straight.** Take a one-handed (left-handed stockman's/ cavalry) grip on the reins and be prepared to quickly adjust (with indirect rein or lower leg) the pony's orientation to a straight spine if it tries to move its hindquarters, head or shoulders off the line required for a safe, straight handover.[33] The picture below shows what can happen if the outgoing rider does not keep their pony straight and moving at the point of handover.

---

32   I prefer to have the handovers occur at a point 2m short of the start line as it gives the riders a little flexibility to adjust their advance if the incoming pony slows quicker than expected. Any further back than 2m gives the opposition a sizeable head start.

33   This is less likely to happen if the outgoing mount is moving freely forward (good timing/judgement) into the handover rather than being restrained when he knows he is about to be put into canter and a two point seat.

Keep the outgoing pony straight and moving forward.

d. **Right hand to the right.** Ensure that the right hand is forward as described above and to the right so that the hand is outside the vertical line of the right stirrup and the elbow is bent to decrease the chance of muscular skeletal injury.

e. **Fingers extended, hand still**. Ensure that the fingers are fully extended with the hand open. The outgoing rider has a responsibility to provide the incoming rider with as big a target as possible. Try not to have the hand move up and down in the vertical plane as it makes it very hard to place the equipment accurately while moving.

f. **Receiving the equipment.** Take a firm, full-handed grip of the equipment and take the arm to the rear (cushion), watching the equipment until it is confirmed as secure in the rider's grip.

g. **Focus on the task and adjust your line.** Look to the first task and adjust the line early to maximise the chance of success at the first task in the field of play in the race.

52. Consistent with the advice provided for incoming riders (at paragraph 50), **do not** ride into the handover with the arm fully stretched to the front (hand near the pony's ear) as this brings the riders too close for comfort/safety. Likewise, **do not** have the arms to the side (90 degrees from the line of movement) as this limits the cushion effect and gives the riders no flexibility to chase the handover if necessary.

VAULTING

53. Vaulting on and off a games pony gives the rider and their team a decided advantage when vaults are executed effectively. These manoeuvres, however, also represent possible causes of short and long term injury, particularly to the spine, so it behoves coaches to ensure that riders are taught the best methods for dismounting and mounting without using stirrups.

Dismounting on the move

54. The moving dismount is used during a quick recovery or as a way of maintaining momentum and control during a race that requires the rider to execute particular actions from the ground, like the Stepping Stone Dash/Agility Aces. The following sequence of actions is recommended to prepare for and execute a safe moving dismount:

    a. **Visualise line and place for dismount.** Before the race starts, visualise the line to be taken and the place for the dismount.

    b. **Identify where to kick feet out of stirrups.** Identify the interim position short of the dismount point where the feet will be kicked out of the stirrups.

    c. **Visualise the dismount and the actions that follow**. Visualise the dismount occurring at the run, with the feet facing forward, and executing the race's requirements while dismounted.

    d. **Launch.** With the envisioned plan in mind, start the race and adjust the line to achieve the planned dismount point.

    e. **Reins in left hand.** Before the chosen stirrup disengagement spot, take the reins in the left hand in a single-handed grip (depending on the pony a half halt may be needed before the stirrups are disengaged).

f.   **Right hand on pommel to take your weight from stirrups.** Place the right hand on the pommel of the saddle and take the body's weight from the stirrups.

g.   **Moving dismount—the action chain.** Withdraw the feet out of the stirrups and, concurrently or immediately after, move the left-handed grip on the reins to the pony's neck (nearer the poll) and release the reins so that they hang freely either side of the pony's neck and can be easily grasped without applying pressure on the neck. With the left hand providing purchase on the neck and the right hand providing a pivot point on the pommel, rock the upper body in a smooth motion forward over the neck and swing the right leg over the saddle. At the start of the downward swing of the right leg, twist the hips slightly to the left to square them with the direction of travel of the pony.

h.   **Landing.** Land running with the left foot in front of the right and, if necessary, using the pommel for stability, not the reins.

A running landing with the left foot in front of the right.

i.   **After landing—the action chain.** At the run, take the nearside rein in the right hand (if executing a nearside dismount) close to the bit, run next to the pony with the upper arm parallel with the ground, the forearm at 90 degrees to the upper arm, facing the direction of travel and the wrist cocked to the right allowing the forearm to be parallel with the pony, but placing the elbow next to the pony's neck to discourage it from pushing the rider to the left off the line of travel.

Stationary vault

55. The stationary vault is used during recoveries or when a rider chooses to dismount over or very close to the equipment and chooses to keep their pony stationary (possibly facing away from the other ponies if the pony has a habit of rushing).

The following sequence of actions assumes that the rider is already dismounted and ready to remount with a nearside vault.

a.   **Preparation—the left hand.** With the equipment in the right hand, slide the left hand between the left rein and the nearside of the pony's neck and take a hold of the saddle (thigh roll, monkey grip or pommel), or take a hold of the pony's mane or neck strap.

b.   **Preparation—the right hand.** Take a grip with the right hand on the pommel or right thigh roll.

c.   **The vault.** While looking at the pony's nearside (left) front hoof (yes—the nearside hoof!) swing the right leg high and back, spring off the left foot and with a high leg lift, swing the right leg over the cantle, at the same time bringing the right hip forward to bring the rider's seat gently into the saddle[34].

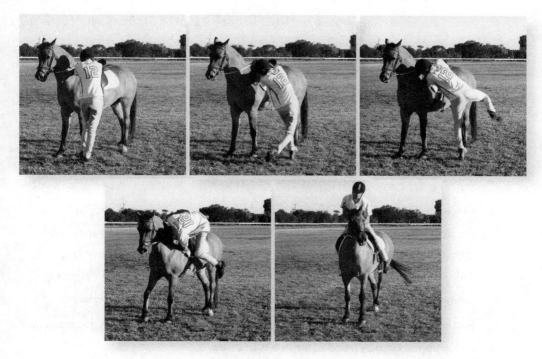

The stationary vault—good head position and gentle into the saddle.

---

34   To achieve the gentle entry into the saddle the rider must take a greater proportion of their weight on the pommel or pony's neck to allow the elegant entry into the saddle. A hard 'dump' onto the saddle hurts the pony and the pony's continued compliance may not be assured if it is constantly hurt by an inconsiderate vaulting technique.

56.   **Training the stationary vault.** Training the rider to execute the stationary vault is like training a young horse to do something new. The action has to be broken into its component parts and conducted slowly at first until the 'muscle memory' starts to make actions smooth and later instinctive.

a.   Start with a pony that is safe, reliable and accustomed to being vaulted onto.

b.   Have a handler hold the pony so it does not move from its optimal position once placed there.

c.   Have an observer conversant with the safe requirements of a standing vault to offer advice and help as it is hard for the handler to observe whether the rider is taking off from behind the wither or not; whether they are swinging their right leg enough or bending their knee as it passes the cantle; or indeed have their head and eyes in the correct orientation to ensure that the spine travels through a natural range of movement etc.

d.   Select a piece of rising ground and have the pony placed on the downhill side and the rider on the nearside, uphill from the pony for a nearside vault.

e.   Have the handler stand on the downhill side with the pony, holding the reins or lead rope short.

f.   Have the rider take a comfortable grip on mane, neck strap, monkey grip or saddle with both hands while the handler steadies the pony.

g.   The rider should practice swinging their right leg up to the height of the saddle while bringing their head down to the pony's shoulder while looking at the nearside hoof.

h.   Once the swinging leg and the torso bend are synchronised it is a matter of having the rider bounce off their left foot, just before the right leg achieves its apex, while taking their body weight in their arms, shoulders, chest and through their stomach, and spring up onto the pony. As the right leg clears the cantle, bring the right hip forward while the legs are being spread and the right leg is bent at the knee.

i.   Ensure the rider lowers their body into the saddle as landing heavily in the saddle will not be appreciated by—and may hurt— the pony.

j.   As the rider's muscle memory and synchronised exertions become more practiced, move the pony to flatter land until the rider can vault on the flat.

Note 1: Remember, the standing vault should be done softly to prevent discomfort to the pony and possibly hurting its back over time.

Note 2: The head position with the eyes looking at the nearside hoof, and the rider's right ear almost touching the pony's nearside shoulder, allows the rider's seat to get into the saddle with the rider's spine going through a natural range of movement. Other techniques, where the rider's eyes are above the wither looking to the offside, force the spine into a constricted twisting movement that can cause injuries if the pony pig-roots or kicks out at a nearby pony at that exposed point in time. (This happened to one of my daughters in training and she sustained a back injury, which led me to analyse the process in detail to find what I consider to be the best vaulting techniques.)

Note 3: This recommended technique, and the associated muscle memory, allows girls who will turn into young women, and whose body shape may change dramatically in their teenage years and beyond, to continue vaulting onto their pony as their centre of gravity and/or power-to-weight ratio change. It is also the best technique for young riders—boys or girls—who lack the upper body strength to haul themselves into the saddle, as older riders (particularly the boys) will do as their bodies mature and their associated power-to-weight ratios change.

Running vault

57. For this exercise to be trained effectively the pony being used to train the rider has to happily trot or canter with the rider running at the pony's shoulder. The running vault is the easiest to learn and takes the least amount of relative strength to execute as it relies on using the momentum of the pony and the pendulum effect of the vault to pull the rider off the ground and allow them to slide into the saddle from a position of some elevation. It does not need long run-ups to execute but it does require the pony to be moving or accelerating from a slower gait. I like to encourage riders with buckled longer reins to unbuckle them and tie a knot in them so the knot is further back than the withers but not too far back. The aim is to have the reins easily gathered after the vault is successfully landed. The steps for executing a sound running vault are as follows:

   a. **Visualise where.** Visualise the race and the position in the lane at which the rider will execute the vault.

   b. **Visualise what follows the vault.** Visualise the actions immediately after the vault has been successfully executed and the rider has full control of the pony (albeit possibly without having feet inside the stirrup irons).

   c. **Preparation.** At the point where the vault is to be executed, and with the pony and rider moving at the run (the rider must not get behind the pony's withers), the rider momentarily drops the rein contact and grips the pony's mane or crest or the saddle/ monkey grip with the left hand, and the pommel of the saddle with the right hand.

d.   **The vault.** Within one or at most two steps the rider springs off of the leading foot (usually the left foot). Some riders like to hold the saddle for a stride and bounce into a two footed take-off similar to vaulting techniques used in riding demonstrations at a circus. To achieve either technique, the rider needs to tense the muscles in their arms, shoulders and stomach as they spring and swing their legs off the ground with an associated spreading of the legs and the right hip moving forward to bring the rider's seat into the saddle smoothly. Again the rider executes the vault looking at the pony's nearside hoof.

The running vault—good control, core strength and coordination, correct head position, and a measure of courage as well.

Note 1: If the rider keeps their head on the left side of the pony's neck while executing the vault, not only does it ensure that the rider's spine travels through a natural range of movement, but in a leading race the pony also protect the rider's head if the leading pony (usually on the offside) decides to kick out at the led pony just as the rider is executing their vault. In my 15+ years of coaching I have only seen this happen once but it scared me enough to convince me that the best place for a rider's head while vaulting is next to the pony's nearside shoulder.

Note 2: It is even more important to control the height from which the rider descends into the saddle. High vaults cause riders to land in the saddle with considerable force and can damage a pony's or a horse's back. The ideal running vault is a skip into the saddle where the right leg barely clears the cantle and the rider slides into their riding position almost unfelt by the pony.

Note 3: There is no contact with either rein for the fraction of a second that it takes to execute the vault. Contact on the reins may encourage the pony to deviate from the best line and may cause obstruction problems if the pony and rider leave their lane[35].

58. **Training the running vault.** Again, learning the running vault should be broken into its component parts, and then bought together when the rider has successfully completed these. A degree of fitness and agility is required for vaults to be executed and some riders may first have to work on their strength, fitness and agility before they can commence practicing with a pony. Depending on the age, strength and fitness of the rider (and sometimes the handler) it might be best to plan several short lessons in which to teach the vault.

59. Training beginners to execute a running vault requires a safe pony that is accustomed to riders vaulting onto it. The pony should be matched to the size of the rider so that a larger rider is not practicing on a small pony which can be injured by a heavy body landing its uncoordinated weight onto the pony's back time after time.

60. It also helps if there is an experienced handler who can run with the pony and vaulting rider to ensure that the rider can build sufficient momentum to execute the vault effectively.

---

35 Usually due to pressure on the left rein as the rider lacks the confidence to trust the pony to run straight. If the rider constantly holds the left rein while vaulting the pony will learn to turn its head into the rider, thereby restricting the available space for the rider to place their head during the vault. This reinforces bad techniques and causes the pony to spin in the vault or drift off the optimal line.

61. It is also advisable to have an observer conversant with the safe requirements of vaulting to offer advice and help as it is hard for the handler to observe whether the rider is taking off from behind the wither or not. Likewise the observer is best placed to see whether the trainee is swinging their right leg high enough or bending their knee as it passes the cantle, or indeed have their head and eyes in the correct orientation to ensure that the spine travels through a natural range of movement. When training the running vault, you may wish to consider the following:

    a.   Choose an open, obstacle-free area where the pony can run freely on a lead rope but where it cannot escape from the rider and handler if it 'gets away'.

    b.   Have the handler on the offside with the trainee vaulter on the nearside and move the pony into a trot.

    c.   Practice the rider gripping the pony or saddle in a manner with which they are comfortable and springing off the ground (with the springing motion of the left foot or a two footed bounce) and holding their weight off the ground for a stride or two of the pony while looking at the pony's nearside hoof.

    d.   When the rider can hold their weight off the ground for a few strides encourage them to spring higher off the ground with a big right leg lift and hip twist as the legs part to accommodate the rider's seat landing in the saddle.

    Note: Remember how hard it was the first time you tried to ride a bike or drive a manual car. Vaulting is not easy, but practice generates muscle memory, and it is the muscle memory that allows the vault to become instinctive in time.

    e.   The rider's head position on the nearside shoulder looking down is critical to injury-free vaulting[36] and soft landings for the pony.

Corner vault

62. The corner vault is used for fast recoveries requiring a change of direction or realignment of the direction being travelled, during such games as Ball and Bucket or Potato Picking Scramble[37], Old Sock/Socks and Buckets, or Tool Box Scramble[38]. The distance from the dismount point to the equipment to be picked

---

36   As explained in Note 2 to paragraph 56, with the rider's head in this position the spine travels through a natural range of movement when vaulting. Looking over the pony's withers during the vault may move the spine through an unnatural range of movement, causing twisting that may lead to injury in some circumstances.

37   No equivalent games for either of these in IMGA.

38   No equivalent Pony Club race.

up will vary from pony to pony but as a general rule the rider should dismount, at speed if possible, with enough distance between them and the equipment for them to get control of their pony in-hand before they get to within 2m of the equipment.

Note: This vault is not for the faint hearted! But it gains at least a half a second (5m to 8m on a fast pony) on competitors who cannot execute the corner vault. This vault takes considerable practice and should only be attempted once stationary and running vaults are mastered.

63. The following considerations are important to achieving a safe and fast corner vault:

    a. **Vaulting experience required as a precondition.** The corner vault requires the vault to be executed while the pony is turning around a stationary (albeit temporarily so) rider. It is the most difficult of the three vaults and should not be considered until riders are vaulting instinctively onto stationary or straight running ponies.

    b. **Prepare by visualising the vault before the game starts.** Before executing a corner vault the rider should visualise the dismount, gaining control of the pony in-hand, changing hands on the reins and stepping over and picking up the equipment involved, turning the pony and lowering its head and shoulders, the vault itself, and what they will do immediately after the successful execution of the vault.

    c. **The dismount.** The dismount and controlling the pony in-hand involve placing the reins high on the pony's neck (to ensure that it feels no pressure until the dismount is finished), dismounting on the run and holding the nearside rein in the right hand near the bit as in the running vault, getting control of the pony and confirming the line required.

    d. **Turning the pony around the equipment.** The rider changes hands on the reins several paces before the equipment on the ground and steps over the equipment. This action involves bringing the left hand across in front of the rider's chest and taking the nearside rein close to the bit in time to slow down and then turn the pony around the equipment.

    e. **Picking up the equipment.** Assuming a right-handed pick-up, picking up the equipment involves the rider stepping over the equipment with a big step to the left, bending the knees and keeping the back straight, which lowers the pony's head and shoulders while it turns around the momentarily stationary rider. While grasping the equipment with the right hand, the left hand turns in an arc from where it was across the right side of the body to the left side, which turns the pony in an arc around the rider. The planted left foot keeps the pony off the remainder of the equipment to ensure that it does not scatter the remaining equipment, thereby ensuring the game is not made harder for subsequent team members.

    f.   **The vault.** The vault occurs as the pony is turning. The rider springs from their pick-up position, with momentary disregard for the reins, into the saddle using the standing vault technique, albeit on a pony that is turning around them rather than stationary.

64.   **Hints to protect the equipment.** If the pony or rider knocks the equipment on the ground and scatters it, it may not affect the rider, but it may well affect their team-mates/subsequent riders by making the race longer or harder if the equipment is scattered or—worse— squashed. It is important to train to keep the ponies off the equipment. Therefore, when training for the corner vault, the rider should practice taking the item of equipment furthest to the left of the pile as they look at it with their back to the start line[39]. If they step over the equipment and take the object furthest to the left of the line, when the pony turns into the rider on the ground there is greater chance of the pony not stepping on or scattering the equipment than if a piece of equipment to the right of the line were selected.

65.   **Training the corner vault.** Training the corner vault involves breaking the vault down into its component parts as indicated above and moving through them sequentially. Riders should not move onto the subsequent step until the current step is executed effectively.

    a.   The dismount should occur as described above with the rider landing at the run with the pony controlled by the right hand on the left rein near the bit.

    b.   As the rider approaches the equipment at the run, when they are just short of the equipment they should change hands on the nearside rein so that the left hand now grips the rein close to the bit.

---

39   Not possible for the Spillers Pole Race where the letters are jumbled, but it is recommended that the rider still plants their left foot to the left of the equipment to ensure that the pony does not get inadvertently pulled onto the equipment.

The corner vault—early dismount, keeping pony off equipment, fast bounce back into saddle.

c.   As the rider steps over the equipment and bends at the knees (preferably with a straight back) to pick up the equipment with the right hand, the left arm/hand swings in an arc to the left[40].

d.   Upon grasping the equipment and when the pony is sufficiently through its turn, the rider lets go of the rein with the left hand and takes their favoured vaulting grip on the pony or saddle and springs into the saddle.

Note 1: It is important not to inadvertently or deliberately put pressure on the left rein when executing the corner vault as this may cause a well-trained pony to veer to the left as it accelerates away from the turn, thereby taking a less favourable line. It also creates a risk of interfering with another rider if the pony runs outside its lane, which may result in elimination from the game. Practice between pony and rider will determine whether the rider needs to spring up early with the pony just starting their turn or a fraction of a second later when the pony has almost completed its turn.

Note 2: It is important to consider the length of rein when vaulting. I don't like 'sporting reins'[41] which dictate a set—usually quite short— length. On the other hand, longer unknotted reins can dangle and loop too far for easy gathering and control immediately after the vault. In preparation for a vaulting race I often recommend that riders unbuckle their reins, then tie a knot in them, ensuring they are still long enough to allow the indirect and opening rein to work for the rider, but without allowing a large loop to form in the reins when the rider is dismounted.

---

40   As mentioned earlier, this has the effect of both turning the pony around the equipment and lowering the pony's head, which drops the withers a few centimetres, making the vault a little easier.

41   Short reins, or more commonly a single rein that attaches to both sides of the bit, that may reach only to the wither. These reins allow neck-reining and stop aids, but provide little or no ability to control the shoulders and only a limited capacity for employment of an opening rein.

Equipment/Tack

66. This section highlights a number of considerations that have proved problematic for me as a coach in the past, and are therefore worth mentioning.

Saddle

67. As for all equestrian disciplines, it is very important that the saddle tree is not broken, that the saddle fits the pony and is off his spine and is not seated too far back on the pony or too far forward on his withers. The saddle should not pull the saddle blanket down on the withers and one should be able to put a vertical hand inside the gullet to confirm this lack of pressure on the pony's spine.

Bridle

68. The bridle should not be so small that the pony's mouth is in contact with both sides of the bit when no pressure is being applied to either rein. Thick bits are arguably uncomfortable for the pony as there is limited space in the mouth if the tongue is naturally seated. I acknowledge that there are many opinions on bits and I suggest that you experiment until you find a fit that works for both pony and rider.[42]

Reins

69. **Short knotted reins.** I do not like short knotted reins as they often limit the ability to apply pressure with the indirect rein to control the shoulders while opening the inside rein to show the pony in clear terms where the rider wants to go. They also encourage a rider to ride one-handed more than they should. Having said this, there are some circumstances where I do recommend them, but they are either with younger riders who are still gaining their balance and rhythm, or older riders about to play a vaulting game where they want to easily re-gather the reins after the vault.

---

42   Please consult your organisation's guidance on which bits are and are not allowed. Both Pony Club and IMGA have strict guidelines on which bits may be used.

70. **Long knotted reins.** Reins knotted 'long' are sometimes necessary in vaulting races so that there is not too much rein hanging down one side for the rider to gather their reins effectively once back in the saddle. The rider and race will dictate if reins need to be knotted long or not.

71. **Sporting reins.** For similar reasons I do not like sporting reins (see Note 2 to paragraph 65 and the associated footnote 41) for mounted games ponies ridden by older/ experienced riders. I find that they limit the rider's options and again make it difficult to communicate with the outside rein. These reins appear to work well for ponies trained to neck rein and for small/young riders, but often the neck-reining pony will turn its head in the direction of intended travel and either fall through the shoulder in that direction, causing balance issues for the rider, or it may swing its hindquarters in the other direction to effect the turn which invariably takes the rider away from the equipment even though the pony's head may be almost on top of it.

Stirrup irons

72. Stirrup irons need to be wide enough for the rider's feet to move in and out of them easily— often before or after a vault. The placement of the stirrup bars or fenders on some stock/ hybrid saddles place the stirrups too close to the pony's forelegs for my liking and they tend to sit the rider in an armchair-like seat, pushing the lower leg even further forward. A rider seated in this position may inadvertently cause the stirrups to come into frequent, uncomfortable contact with the pony's legs/elbows/shoulders (depending on the length of the rider's legs). This can confuse the pony as to the required response to the inadvertent 'aid', can create control issues due to this confusion, and can lead to the type of calcification injuries sometimes seen where spurs are used incessantly on a horse's ribcage.

Breast plates

73. I like breast plates on the ponies I coach, both because they help to stop saddles slipping completely under the pony if a rider has not paid sufficient attention to the girth tension and because, when things are happening quickly for a rider, there are several extra points of grip that can be used for balance or leverage.

THE GAMES

Define the field of play

74. When conducting training for a team or individuals I have found it best if you can define an area in which you expect the riders to ride. This should be clearly defined with road cones, bunting, a fence, a hedge or a combination of the above. After a while the ponies get used to working in these confines, which helps in maintaining a safe lesson/practice session. I prefer to choose an area that is not subject to visual or auditory distractions for the riders or ponies. In training areas or practice areas that are large, I use hand signals to convey to the riders the messages 'come to me please'[43], 'line up in line-abreast formation'[44] or 'line up in a horseshoe formation.'[45] This saves my voice and gets the riders used to being attentive to my lesson.

Equipment considerations

75. The following are some equipment-related considerations that may be of benefit to the new coach when approaching a season of coaching and competing with a mounted games team:

---

43   At the risk of being considered a 'military moron' I have adopted this from the infantry field craft guide. This signal is conveyed using one hand raised above the head and lowered so the extended inside of the hand is lowered onto the top of the head and then raised and lowered (similar to a patting movement) so that the movement attracts the rider's attention.

44   Once the riders are on the move towards me I give the signal for the formation I would like them to adopt to make it easier to discuss teaching points from the last run or to demonstrate a particular technique at a particular piece of equipment. The signal for line abreast is two arms extended and the riders are expected to place themselves in a single line facing me with the centre of the team line within easy speaking distance of me.

45   The horseshoe formation is usually used on larger groups or on windy days and the signal is delivered with the upper arms extended as for the line abreast request but the forearms angled in towards where you require the riders, i.e. at 90 degrees to the upper arms, thereby forming a U shape with the upper arms and torso.

a.   **It must be safe.** The fundamental consideration with the equipment is that it
should not increase the dangers or risks in the race/game.

b.   **No square edges, painted**. There should be no, or minimal, square edges and
any timber used should be sanded and painted/covered to ensure that no-one
gets splinters in their hands or legs from contacting the equipment.

c.   **Easy and safe to place and store**. The weight and compact characteristics
of the equipment need to be considered for placement or ease of storage,
movement and handling without heightened potential for muscular-skeletal
or manual handling injuries to the equipment helpers.

d.   **Keep it the same as your team will use in competition.** Equipment used
for training or practice should be similar if not the same as that being used in
competitions. Having said that, however, I often commission the production
of equipment that is harder to handle/negotiate as I follow the old military
tradition of 'train hard—fight easy'. In this case, it is more accurate to say 'train
hard—play easy'.[46]

---

46   I prefer bending poles that fall over easily if knocked so that the riders and ponies learn to stay off them.
I like the practice hurdles and tyres to be smaller than the actual specifications so that, when the team
gets to the competition, the equipment appears easy.

GENERAL RULES

76. It is very important for riders who intend to perform mounted games at the higher levels to know the rules for each game intimately. It is also advisable for them to know the general rules associated with competitions so that the team is not disadvantaged by an ill-informed choice by one of the riders in the field of play. Teams that are serious about their training will sometimes conduct theory lessons for new riders to ensure that all riders understand the actions to be taken if equipment is knocked or placed incorrectly, or if equipment is damaged or knocked into/out of the field of play, etc.

77. During a competition it is important to remember that the line stewards are there to support the Technical Delegate/Referee[47]. If a rider leaves the arena not having corrected a mistake or not having realised a mistake has been made, the team will/ should be eliminated. So riders need to know the rules and what 'doing it right' looks like. They need to know how to fix a problem because in some games the rider's hands cannot correct the equipment but the equipment can be used to adjust position (see the rules for the Pyramid Race[48]).

78. When young riders ride in teams with more experienced riders it is often a good practice to have the experienced and therefore more knowledgeable rider designated as the caller for the race. The caller can then advise on actions in the race to ensure that the rules are applied and the team is not eliminated. In Pony Club events coaches are not usually allowed to give instructions once the race has

---

47   Technical Delegate is the term used in Pony Club for the person responsible for the conduct of the championship/competition and the implementation of all rules. That person's equivalent in the IMGA is called the Referee.

48   The IMGA Association Race is very similar to the Pony Club Pyramid Race but IMGA does allow such hand contact—so please consult local rules.

started, so a caller with a good knowledge of the rules and how they are going to be applied is an asset to a team.

79. Before a competition it is normal for the team coaches/managers to meet with the Technical Delegate/Referee to clarify how the rules will be interpreted for the races/games being played. This meeting should also allow the teams to inspect the equipment, as equipment can change from region to region or country to country.

80. For riders competing in both Pony Club and IMGA events it is important to understand the differences in the rules. While the differences are sometimes subtle, riders can be eliminated in an IMGA competition for doing something that is allowed in Pony Club competition. A case in point is the re-erection of equipment if it has been knocked over. In Pony Club competitions there is no need to replace the equipment on the same spot from where it was dislodged, but in IMGA there is a mark on the ground where, say, a cone needs to sit, and if any part of that cone is not touching or over the spot, the rider is eliminated after the race with no discussion entered into. So ensure that you take the time to discuss and teach the rules.

Riding skills

81. Coaches are advised to refer to Dr Andrew McLean's works for consistency in horse training in-hand and under saddle. The most important aspect of riding in mounted games is for both the pony and rider to be balanced at all times. I strongly recommend dressage training for all my riders and I like to see that their heels are lower than their toes in the stirrups and that they have steady lower legs, square shoulders and are looking up, in the upright seat, the three point seat and the two point seat. I acknowledge that this short description is but scratching the theoretical and practical surface of what is required to master the following, but I hope it conveys the importance of seeking additional guidance from riding instructors to help train the pony and rider to achieve the necessary control to make riding games both enjoyable and safe. The following skills are very important to achieve a good mounted games combination of the pony and rider.

Balance

82. Good balance requires the ability to direct and use the correct diagonals and leads, which allows the pony to remain balanced throughout the manoeuvres required of the game. This does not imply balance in the sense of a rider who, while out of synchronisation with the pony, still has the ability to get the job done without falling off. That, to me, is risky behaviour in terms of the health and safety of the rider and pony, as well as the team, as the chance of that rider making a mistake while 'unbalanced' with their pony is much greater than a good upright or two/three point seat.

83. The position of the rider's head and hands will influence balance. A rider who has their hands immobile in close vicinity to the pommel of the saddle will almost invariably have hunched shoulders and their head will be looking down.

To reach optimal balance the rider should have their hands forward of the withers, slightly apart with the fingers forward taking light pressure through the reins, with bridged reins or reins in a single-handed grip and the head looking up in the direction of intended travel, such that the rider should be able to feel the collar of their shirt with the back of their neck.

Flexing

84. Flexing involves the ability to flex the pony's head to either the left or right from the upright seat, which allows a balanced approach to equipment without losing control of the hindquarters, the loss of which can take equipment out of reach at a critical point in the race. To flex the pony to the left, the left rein pressure needs to be constant and, in the early stages of training, open (wide away from the pony's neck). The right rein maintains pressure but is closed on the neck while its length is adjusted (slightly longer) to allow the flexion.

85. It is important that the rider does not attempt to achieve flexion by moving the outside rein (in the example above this would be the left rein) past the point of the withers. Again, flexing the pony should be able to be achieved with light rein pressure. Some trainers will also recommend maintaining leg pressure on the girth to turn the pony around that contact or push it to the equipment.

Leg yielding

86. Leg yielding is the ability to yield the pony's hindquarters to the offside or nearside with lower leg pressure from one side at a time only (the opposite to the direction required i.e, if you require the pony's quarters to move left, the right leg is used to apply pressure behind the girth). This, among other manoeuvres, is important for good control at the back of the changeover box to keep ponies and riders facing forward while moving their mounts to the right to make room for the incoming rider to join the team without having to venture into the lane of the team next to them.

87. The pony should be trained to move away from pressure, not just in response to the backwards movement of the rider's leg (i.e. before pressure is applied). Ponies that 'yield' when the leg moves back but before pressure is applied are actually evading the contact and need further training as they will usually rush the canter transition, which is not good for the rider. This is, however, fairly easily fixed in the dressage arena.

Steering

88. Much steering in mounted games is done by keeping the pony between the rider's legs with even and equal pressure of the lower legs. The best steering of the pony occurs before the control zone and is often achieved with two hands on the reins and the pony yielding to leg pressure and 'drifting' to the optimum line of approach by the use of uneven lower leg pressure. Additional pressure from the rider's left leg will drift the pony to the offside/right to achieve the optimal line of approach for the next activity in the game. This can be supported by an opening rein to indicate the line the rider wants the pony to take while the opposite rein retains contact at the shoulders to achieve the 'drift', rather than have the pony bend its neck and swing its hindquarters away from the optimum line. If the pony is cantering or galloping the drift should be achieved from the two point seat with leg pressure at the girth, not behind it.

The downwards transition

89. Many actions on the mounted games arena require the rider to exploit a hoon zone with a view to slowing down or changing direction dramatically at a distant point. To ensure best control in the control zone it is important to adopt a three point seat where the rider's seat is planted in the saddle and the rider's hips and seat move in synchronisation with the pony's movements, leading to the upright seat for the final phase of the equipment-related manoeuvre. No daylight should be seen between the saddle and the rider while exercising this sort of games-related downward transition.

Stopping/halting

90. The ability to stop/halt a pony from any speed and keep it straight and calm is what gives good games-riding combinations an enormous advantage. Good training of the stop/halt aids in the pony/rider combination allows the rider to recover from a mistake with minimum distance and time lost, and allows a longer hoon zone, which brings time benefits to the team. Unlike in some Olympic disciplines, the voice can and should be used as an aid and it should precede the use of physical aids (half halt and halt aids) by a hoofbeat or two, which will usually make for softer use of the bit and a happier pony. Imperative to achieving good stops/halts is keeping the leg still below the hips, the heels

below the balls of the feet in the stirrups and a deep (planted) seat, looking up and not slumped forward. Like the other skills, training to achieve good stops/ halts should be done slowly at first and then the speed increased as the pony and rider become more competent and synchronised.

Note 1: The length of the control zone will be most influenced by the ability of the pony and rider combination to stop/halt. Those combinations that can stop/halt well from an active canter/gallop can use longer hoon zones than those who have a longer stopping distance.

Note 2: Coaches need to impress on riders an understanding of their abilities as they relate to the team. A well-exercised halt or check from a longer control zone is better than a fast attempt with a small control zone that goes wrong.

Note 3: While we talk of training the pony to stop/halt, in competition the actions that precede the stop—the transition down and/or the half halt—are often sufficient for the rider to bleed off enough speed to allow the task to be achieved with momentum. If, however, a recovery is required, a pony that is accustomed to stopping promptly on request is an enormous asset to a games team.

Note 4: Teaching a young rider to halt their pony takes time and, in particular, teaching the rider to stay upright with heels lower than toes during the transition to halt is important. Young riders can fall into an easy habit of pulling back on the reins and allowing their feet to slide forward of the girth in an attempt to give themselves more leverage on the pony's mouth. This is counterproductive as it raises the seat from the saddle and makes it easier for the pony to ignore the rider or attempt other evasion techniques to relieve itself of the pressure/pain caused in its mouth. Coaches should teach young riders to keep their seat planted in the saddle—no daylight should show between the saddle and the rider's seat when executing a downwards transition to halt (this takes some flexibility in the lower back and hips to stay 'in synch' with the movement of the pony while staying upright and 'with' the pony). Rob Bennett, a mentor of mine, used to tell his riders to go home and do 'a million transitions' to get control of the pony in that vital safety control—the downwards transition to halt. As with all training, start these transitions from a slow gait and gradually work up to the transition down from the canter. Aim for a halt within three strides of the given gait.

Half halts

91. The half halt allows the rider to convey to the pony that they are about to do something and to await the next command/request. It is often used to check or bleed off speed from an approach to a control zone to allow a balanced transition down, or to impose a short interruption to the pony's momentum to give the rider a fraction more time to successfully execute a task.

Back-up

92. The back-up is not used as often as it could be in games. Riders often prefer to turn a pony rather than stop it and back it up to the point where they can recover or correct a fault. Given that the back-up is often associated with training the stop or halt, its utility in games could be better exploited.

Parking the pony

93. Earlier I referred to Dr Andrew McLean and his use of 'parking' a horse as a critical aspect of teaching the horse good ground manners, which also helps with overshadowing techniques when training a horse. A pony that you can 'park' is an asset when a rider has to dismount and can trust the pony to stand until it receives the aid to go as dictated by the rider.

GENERIC SKILLS

Selecting the best line for the race

94. Selecting the best line for the race occurs before the race when the rider, with the full knowledge of their pony's capabilities, visualises the race in terms of hoon zones, control zones and the optimum approach to the equipment or task in the control zone. With that image in mind the rider then does their best to keep to those lines for best results. When deviations from the optimum line occur, having a clear mental picture of the best line will allow fast and decisive actions by the rider to still bring in a good time for their leg of the race.

Drifting the horse onto the optimum line

95. When a rider realises early that their present line is not the optimal line, they should make subtle changes to their line to correct the error so as to realign themselves onto the optimum line before they reach the next control zone. This allows a rider to employ their riding skills and drift their pony onto the optimum line they need. It assumes, however, that the rider has sufficient situational awareness to realise early that they are not on the best line and can then allow sufficient time and space to fix the line gently without the use of heavy-handed rein aids that 'punish' the pony for what was fundamentally a rider error.

The dink

96. The 'dink' is a colloquial Australian expression used to describe a manoeuvre, used upon entering the control zone, that allows the rider to bleed off some speed, get control of the pony and alter the line of approach to encourage the pony to drop the shoulder which is closest to the task or equipment. Imagine the letter 'S' described on the ground in the control zone with the middle of the S being

the location of the task or equipment. Assuming the rider is right-handed, the rider approaches the task or equipment on a line to the right of the middle of the lane by at least 2m, and a few metres before the task or equipment they execute a short left turn. At the task or equipment they change back to a right turn. As the pony adjusts to its new line past the task or equipment, it drops its right shoulder slightly and effectively takes a longer line past the equipment than if it had run straight past it. The dink is particularly helpful for riders on unfamiliar ponies or for riders on bigger horses.

The dink—maintaining momentum by taking a slightly longer line.

97. Often good riders will approach a dink in the two point seat and at the point of first turn they readjust the reins and take the three point seat for a pace or two to confirm their synchronised movement with the pony. Just before the point of execution the rider adopts the upright seat and executes the action with the equipment while leaning slightly over the right shoulder. With little encouragement from the indirect rein (left rein) or the inside rein (the right rein) the pony will straighten down the centre of the lane, and in so doing drop that inside shoulder, effectively taking the rider a couple of inches (about 5cm) closer to the equipment.

Picking up equipment—reaching down

98. The first thing I like to train into my riders is not to snatch at the equipment when attempting to pick it up. Also I advise them strongly not to lean out on the pony to effect the pick-up, but to lean slightly to the front and down, with a shift of weight above the pony to keep the centre of balance consistent for the mount. For a right-handed rider, for example, this involves putting weight in the left stirrup, shifting the hips slightly to the left in the two point position, while reaching to the right to pick up the equipment[49]. It also requires the rider to have a good one-handed grip on the reins before leaning down and that the rider should be prepared to engage the left hand actively to ensure that the pony maintains its line and does not rush as the rider changes their point of balance slightly

Good pick up without overreaching, by letting the pony carry the rider to the equipment

---

49   More athletic riders on bigger horses may start their reach-down manoeuvre like this, then actually switch their weight to the right, move their hips to the right so that their buttocks lower, closer to their ankle, while at the same time that foot moves slightly under the horse's chest. This allows for a long reach down and a controlled one-legged lift back into the saddle. One young rider explains this technique as 'sitting on your ankle'. Note that this technique still does not involve leaning out from the horse and risking unbalancing it.

when reaching down[50]. Riders should also be aware that any increased or decreased leg pressure on the pony might cause an adverse reaction if the pony is not sufficiently trained. When picking equipment up at speed it is advisable to take the equipment with a back-lifting action. This reduces the effect of forward momentum and allows a softer pick up. Effectively the back-lifting action while the pony and rider are moving forward aims to keep the equipment stationary in the vertical plane.

Putting down equipment—reaching down

99.   Putting equipment down securely at speed takes a lot of practice, good hand-eye coordination and good riding. Again, I train my riders to take as much speed out of the action as possible. This is achieved by reaching forward with the equipment and placing it in or on the correct spot with a rearwards and downwards placing motion. This usually relies on the hand moving down in the vertical plane at the same time it is moving back in the horizontal plane. The effect is a rearward put-down of the equipment which is aimed at softening the placement while effectively maintaining forward momentum as the rider places the equipment. The pictures below show a rider bringing her new games horse to a stop while she reaches down—holding the bottom of the bottle with good technique to stabilise it as she pulls her hand away with a rearward motion.

Good work on a green horse.

Turning tightly around a table or barrel

100. The ability to turn around a table or barrel and be close enough to pick up or put down a piece of equipment is a skill that relies on the rider being able to drift the pony onto the best line and keep it there with lower legs and a single hand on the reins at the moment of placement or pick-up of the equipment.

---

50   An active left rein in this situation could be direct pressure or it could be as light as a vibration to remind the pony that contact could be used if needed.

Turning around equipment at speed—good line of approach, control and technique.

101. I train my riders to ride a line that passes the table or barrel by a metre or so into the changeover box before executing the turn. Yes, this makes the race perhaps 2m longer than for the rider who turns tightly around the table or barrel, but it gives my riders free ground in which to turn the pony and confirm the line before reaching down to barrel height. It allows the line to be achieved with two hands on the reins, thereby employing the outside rein to hold the shoulders. It allows for the upright seat to check and keep the pony balanced and allows it to be moving in a straight line when the rider leans forward at the pony's shoulder to put down or pick up the equipment. I find this technique reduces the risk of the pony knocking the table or barrel.

Soft hands

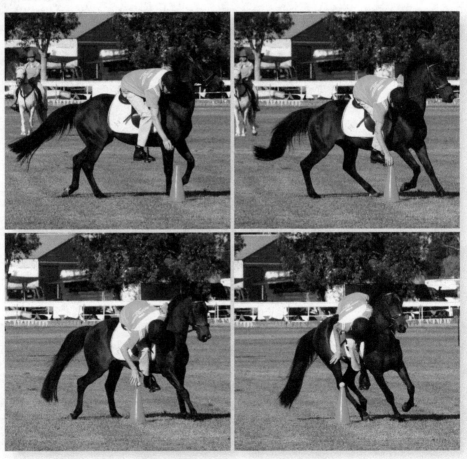

Soft hands at work with the lightest touch – equipment stationary in the vertical plane.

102. Riders who pick up or put down equipment with good back-lift or rearwards placing motion are often referred to as having soft hands. Effectively, such riders have the ability to keep the equipment stationary in the vertical plane while moving past the equipment, often at speed. Riders without soft hands can be heard putting equipment down as the moving equipment meets the stationary equipment, or are often seen knocking over stationary equipment like poles, cones or tables because they imparted too much force on the stationary object for it to stay stationary.[51]

Leading another rider's horse

103. In Australian Pony Club and IMGA competitions it is acceptable to lead a pony by holding both reins. In The Pony Club in Great Britain this would incur elimination. It is imperative that coaches and riders clarify the rules and their local interpretation before the games training season begins. Games that require one rider to lead another mostly involve vaulting and teams choose specific techniques and tactics as a time saving mechanism. There is no doubt that the rider leading the dismounted rider's pony can have a most positive influence on the game if they lead the other pony well. The following points should be considered when leading a dismounted rider's pony.

   a. **Mounted rider to first identify and ride the optimum line.** Before the mounted rider takes their team mate's pony's reins, they must identify the optimum line to take and ride that line.

   b. **Dismounting rider to move reins forward.** The dismounting rider can help the leading rider by moving the reins of the led pony up to its poll just before the dismount to ensure a loop in the reins below the led pony's head. This ensures that when the leading rider takes the rein/s behind the bit, there is no pressure on the led pony's neck which can cause some ponies to stop.

   c. **Mounted rider to control own pony one-handed**. The mounted rider must take control of their own pony with one hand on the reins and have a sufficiently tight grip to ensure the reins do not lengthen during that part of the race where the rider cannot adjust the rein length.

   d. **Marry-up before dismount.** The marry-up with the other rider is to occur before the rider dismounts.

---

51   I like to train my riders with polystyrene cups on bending poles as they break easily and let the rider know with no uncertainty that they have been too heavy on the equipment.

e.   **Essential actions by leading rider.** The leading rider needs to do three things concurrently while the dismounted rider is performing their ground based task. They need to:

(1) Talk to the dismounted rider so that the dismounted rider can judge the location and speed of the rider and the two mounts.

(2) Control the speed and line of approach so that when the dismounted rider is ready to mount they only have to turn their shoulder to the right and their pony's saddle is within easy grasping distance for the vault.

(3) Before the dismounted rider vaults onto their pony, the leading rider needs to leg yield their pony's hindquarters away from the led pony to ensure that the vaulting rider has room to lower their right leg between the two ponies to execute a safe vault. This has the added benefit of discouraging the leading pony from kicking out at the led pony, which can happen in the heat of the moment.

FOR COACHES

Understanding how the brain works

104. **Dave's Story.** I came to riding after my football days concluded. I was 38 years old and I could not keep up with the 18 year olds anymore and I would take until the following Thursday to be rid of the aches and stiffness. I coached junior mounted games teams for six years before I overcame my expected embarrassment at being 'flogged' by my teenage team members in open mounted games competitions. Mounted games are great fun and over the years I have experienced things as a rider that have helped me understand a coach's challenge better.

105. For example, only recently a good friend of mine joined me at the national AMGA pairs championships where we were entered in the Veterans class. (This is a standing joke with those of us older than 40 or 50 as to qualify to be a veteran in the AMGA a rider has to be over 25!) So my mate Mark and I found ourselves in sharp competition. One race we fronted up for was the Three-Legged Sack Race[52] (where one rider starts with a potato sack and rides to the changeover end where the second rider is dismounted, hands the sack over, the first rider dismounts, then both riders place one leg in the sack and run back the 60m like a church picnic three-legged race leading the horses). We had not trained together before the competition, but how hard can a sack race be?

106. I positioned myself at the changeover end and rehearsed the game in my mind as the race started. I saw myself taking the bag from Mark, opening it with a skillful flourish, placing my right foot in the bag and by then Mark would have dismounted and come around me and my horse, put his left leg in the bag and we would obviously sprint down the arena and win the race.

---

52   This race is no longer in the IMGA rule book, and there is no Pony Club equivalent race.

107. Working against this plan, and unknown by my conscious mind, was my subconscious mind that took over, and because I put my left leg first into my trousers every morning of my life, under the pressure of the race, I put my left leg in and then when Mark came to put his left foot and leg in the sack he looked at me with a mixture of surprise and sympathy obviously thinking 'Dave's losing it— he can't tell left from right, poor old bugger'.

108. After the race I apologised to Mark and we had a laugh and recalled many similar occasions where riders we had coached had done similar things. I thought about this.

109. Earlier in the year I had attended a safety conference where several of the speakers talked on the topic of neuro plasticity—the brain's ability to fix itself and other interesting concepts. We, people, become very comfortable with habits and our subconscious mind will kick in, interpret things it is used to seeing or doing—so naturally when I was under pressure and had to place a leg in the sack quickly, the left one went in there because I could do that quickly, because I practice that movement every day. Thinking on this I became aware that I needed to re-examine how I trained my teams because I may actually be limiting their instinctive options by not practicing for the 'unexpected'.

Training Techniques

110. **Repetitive training technique.** I have spent most of my coaching time using repetition as my principle technique as I wanted the riders to achieve a degree of muscle memory for the tasks we/they need to do instinctively. This is an excellent approach for young riders but I have found that it lets some riders down as they, for example, may drop a piece of equipment from their right hand and dismount from the nearside and have to move under the pony's neck to pick up the object then duck under the pony's neck for a second time in two seconds and mount/vault on the nearside because that is the side from which they practice mounting and dismounting most frequently. Clearly the fastest way to recover this piece of equipment is to conduct an offside dismount—pick up the equipment and mount on the offside—saving at least two seconds. But under pressure many riders will have dismounted and commenced ducking under the pony's neck for the first time before they have actually thought about what is to come next—the subconscious and practiced dismounting neural pathways had kicked in and habit had won over expediency. Just like me with the left foot in the sack instead of the right foot.

111. **Reactive training techniques.** The repetitive technique provides an outstanding basis for a perfect game plan. When everything goes to plan, the approach will adopt the perfect line, the momentum and speed will be optimal for the pony and rider combination and the rider's mastery of the appropriate technique will see the equipment used as envisaged and the remainder of the equipment left perfect for the next rider. When the race does not go perfectly is when riders have to be able to adapt their envisaged plan and to adjust to a new plan which accommodates the imperfect situation with which they are now presented. I now ask my riders to approach objects and situations left-handed/using the non-master hand. I get them to dismount and mount from the offside as often as they do the nearside. I aim to train the brain to not get in a habit of always doing something one way as I think this will let down a rider when at a high level of competition /performance they will inadvertently revert to an action that will not be the percentage play on that occasion. Ideally, I would like to commence this type of combined repetitive and reactive training with riders while they are young (under 12) so that by the time they are on fast ponies/horses they are used to adapting a technique to fit the circumstances they find which may or may not be perfect or as envisaged when waiting for the game to start.

112. **Swapping horses.** I also like to have my riders swap horses with other riders in the team so that they have to appreciate the control techniques of other horses. Often they gain a new appreciation of the skills of their team mates when they have to ride a pony with which they have not formed habitual behaviours and responses. A note of caution is warranted here. Ensure that the combinations are workable, the parents agree and, if at a Pony Club sanctioned training day, the organisation has agreed in advance of the training and that training is taken slowly until you are happy the combinations are safe. If training as part of pony club activities this may not be allowed under some club rules so please check local guidelines or seek advice before using the horse swap technique to stimulate multiple neurological responses in your riders.

Fitness to train

113. **Confirming rider fitness.** Before commencing a training session it is important for the coach to know if any of the riders have any injuries before the training session starts. Commonly a rider may have pre-existing conditions which may

have to be taken into account on the day to ensure that they do not aggravate the injury. Coaches should both talk to the riders to confirm this and be on the lookout for early signs of a rider who is not comfortable and again 're-appreciate' the training given to that rider if serious enough to ensure that the rider recovers as soon as possible.

114. **Confirming pony fitness.** Confirming the fitness of the ponies presented for training is a little more difficult as you also do not want to aggravate an injury to a pony or maltreat the animal for which you have responsibility during the training session, but the pony must be observed closely to ascertain its fitness. Old ponies that are safe for young riders may have arthritis and it will be a judgement call between the coach and the parents as to whether the pony is in pain and its retirement should be considered. Watch for an uneven gait or the bobbing of the head which will often indicate discomfort. Look closely at the unmounted pony, both while being led at walk and trot. Ask the person leading the pony to turn the pony in a rather tight turn and see if the added pressure on the inside hoof, leg or shoulder causes a bobbing of the head or a flinching in its stride. A pony should not be ridden if it is lame and it should not be drugged to deaden the pain for it to pass a fitness check in competition. As a coach I always identified a spare pony for the team and we brought that pony to training sessions and everyone practiced on it so that if it was needed at short notice riders had an idea of its idiosyncrasies before the championship and the other ponies were comfortable in its company.

PREPARING A TEAM FOR COMPETITION

Selecting best horse and rider combinations for the race

115. Depending on the race, the relationship between the ponies in the team, and sometimes the physical and athletic attributes of the riders, will determine combinations in terms of who goes first, second, third, fourth or fifth (on the ground). These combinations will need to be adjusted and practiced to arrive at the best combinations for a particular race[53]. (For example, in Windsor Castle I will often have my smallest pony as the fourth horse/ rider combination so that the rider has the best chance of picking the ball out of the bucket while still mounted. I also like to have the biggest horses at position one or two as the rider is working with equipment about 1m off the ground.)

Note: As a coach you should always have a reason or reasons in every game why the team has a particular order.

Visualising the game

116. Having each rider visualise their 'perfect race' before the game helps to settle the rider, focus their attention on the game and allow them to concentrate for the one to two minutes that the game takes to run. It takes practice and some riders are able to do this better than others.

'Ride your own race'

117. It is important to drill into the riders during training that each rider should not be distracted by the teams in the other lanes, but to concentrate on their own race. Being aware of the unfolding situation using peripheral vision is important, but the rider in play should get assistance from the team's designated caller.

---

53 This assumes that the team intends to give their best performance on the day of competition. Some teams participate purely for social reasons and these considerations therefore may be irrelevant if optimum performance is not a goal for the team.

Developing situational awareness will come with experience, but riders need to know when they have to give the game their 100% attention and when they can update their situational awareness (i.e. in a hoon zone).

The team caller

118. The situational awareness of the rider in play is also the responsibility of the team. I like to have one rider designated as the team's caller with an alternate identified and practiced for those times when the caller is in play. The caller does not give a running commentary or be a cheer leader. The caller assists the rider in play by letting them know the effects of other events unfolding around the rider. Calls like 'they have dropped it, take it easy' take the pressure off the rider in play and allow them to take a more conservative line to the activity/equipment. Likewise, the fifth rider, when dismounted in a game, is ideally suited to take on that role. This assumes of course that the rules allow the fifth rider to communicate—be aware that some games do not allow this.

The difference between riding heats and finals in competition

119. In competitions where finalists are decided based on times there is a fundamental difference in the approach a team should take to heats and finals, compared to competitions where the first two or three teams from the heat qualify for a final.

   a.   In a timed heat[54], the serious teams should be totally focused on achieving the best time, which means riding optimal lines, making no or only minor mistakes, recovering quickly, nailing good handovers and finishing the race well, regardless of where the other teams are in adjacent lanes.

   b.   In a final the aim is to finish in as high a place as possible. I like to aim for second place, which takes the stress off the team. I like to have my most dependable rider go first and my second and third riders my best handover exponents. Each rider is to ride their own race with the aim of gradually establishing and then maintaining a lead. The last rider's role is to maintain the team's place (no death or glory riding). The aim is to conserve the mounts and to keep them as fresh as possible for the last final.

---

54   This appears to be a practice only in Australian Pony Club. After seeing the use in heats of 'first-past-the-post' as the qualifying criterion to progress to the finals in the UK in 2010 I believe this is a fairer and better process. I'd prefer to trust the human eye in determining placings than rely on the potential vagaries of stopwatches and timing.

Recoveries—plan for and practice them

120. In mounted games when a rider makes the race longer, sometimes referred to as a mistake, I like to console my riders by saying 'it happens'. The immediate problem is not that the rider has missed their line or dropped a piece of equipment; the issue from the team perspective is: how quickly can the rider recover? A good deep riding seat, and well trained pony that can stop and back up to light aids, ridden by a rider who is practiced in offside and nearside dismounts, and standing, corner or running vaults, can recover a situation quickly. Often in a final, teams put enormous pressure on themselves and mistakes happen that were not evident in the heats. In these circumstances the team that can consistently recover quickly will have an advantage over the teams that do not have such quick recoveries. In training, therefore, use the inevitable 'mistakes' as opportunities to practice quick, controlled recoveries.

Teamwork

121. Mounted games as played by Pony Clubs, and in pairs and teams in IMGA competitions, rely on good teamwork within the team for it to reach its potential in competition and socially. Solid teamwork is based on a combination of self-respect and self-discipline, respect for others (including the horses) and collective or group discipline. Of the teams I have observed over the years I have been involved with mounted games, the teams that consistently compete with no or only few personnel changes over the years are the teams where the relationships within the team are based on deep mutual respect, both as people and riders.

Managing nervous tension within the team

122. As a coach your influence in a game finishes once the team enters the arena. The techniques and hints above can give the team confidence that their preparation has been as good as time and the team's availability for practice have allowed. Because there is tension before and during a race it is important for all riders to respect each other and be friends. Team building activities like training sessions, theory sessions or just hanging-out after or before training, can be important for the team's cohesion and its ability to manage the tension.

123. My oldest daughter used to lead a song with her team as they rode into the arena to take up their ready position and that often helped the team members and perhaps the ponies cope with the tension generated by the competition.

CONCLUSION

Life skills

124. I acknowledge that it is very hard to put an 'old head on young shoulders' but that is what I love about mounted games. They are a wonderful avenue for young and not-so-young riders to experience life's realities, and I believe they have the potential to build positive and lifelong friendships; as well as building resilience into riders who take their games seriously and who respect their horses, who demonstrate good manners and sportsmanship, and who appreciate the help they receive from the coaches and parents who make it possible for them to participate in mounted games.

Fun

125. Mounted games are designed to be both rewarding and fun. When selecting teams for junior riders, remember that if you want the young rider to continue, it must be fun. I am often asked: 'What is the best way to select a team?' My answer is that within reason, the riders should select with whom they ride i.e. their friendship groups. I watched one of my children lose interest in mounted games because of the people she was told would be in her team and it was never going to be fun for her. Please remember that mounted games, while they can be taken seriously, first and foremost have to be fun for the riders. I have also found that if they are fun for the riders they are also a lot of fun for the support crews who mark the arenas, place the equipment, adjudicate, score, or just provide moral support or transport. If the riders are not enjoying themselves these wonderful volunteers ask themselves, 'Why are we putting our time into mounted games if it isn't fun?'

It must be fun!

Feedback

126. I would like to stress that the methods described here may not be the best or most efficient ways of practicing the games or the skills that are part of mounted games techniques. They do however, represent the considered practices of someone (me) who has studied mounted games from several perspectives, and I am confident that the techniques and processes described above are not wrong—they work and ensure safety margins are built into training techniques and practices. I am, however, happy to concede that other coaches and riders may have different approaches.

127. I would very much like to hear from those coaches and riders who have different and/or better, safe ways of conducting mounted games. If you would like to share your thoughts and consideration with a view to us collaboratively improving the resources available to budding coaches and riders, please feel free to contact me through the web page, or my G Mail account (d.h.equestrianmountedgames@gmail.com) and if your suggestion resonates with me as a safe alternative that could offer another perspective, I will be happy to add your suggestion to the resource pack with appropriate attribution and recognition.

ADDITIONAL RESOURCES FOR COACHES, INSTRUCTORS AND ADMINISTRATORS

128. In accordance with my desire to help coaches and Pony Club instructors, I have developed six lesson plans and two risk management tools which I am sure are not perfect, but I believe they represent a good start point from which I would be very happy if they were adopted and adapted to better suit your situation and circumstances. If this saves you half an hour of lesson preparation time before your rally or training session, or assists in the consideration for an activity you may be responsible for conducting, I will feel that I have helped.

129. The first lesson plan is the Safe Handover/Pass-off lesson plan as this is seen as a fundamental skill and its successful completion by the riders should be a pre-condition to their attempt at the other lessons/games.

130. Lesson plans have been included for the following five fun games[55]:

    a.   Five Flag Race / Flag Fliers
    b.   Hi/Lo Race / HiLo
    c.   Stepping Stone Dash / Agility Aces
    d.   Tack Shop Race[56]
    e.   Old Sock Race / Socks and Buckets

131. I have also included a gallery of photographs with comments that support specific paragraphs in the book to give greater understanding of the techniques and lines of approach used, and these are able to be downloaded from the book's website for free. They offer a strobe-like view of an activity if viewed consecutively with minimum time between exposures. They also offer the ability to enlarge a particular part of the photograph for greater fidelity. It is hoped that in some instances in the handover section for instance that details in the 'back-shot' will be as informative as the foreground details.

---

55   Please note the difference in the Pony Club names for the races (first mentioned) and the IMGA name for a very similar race. See local guides for equipment and other differences.

56   There is no IMGA equivalent of the Tack Shop Race.

132. Additional safety material that may be helpful and which is offered as a start point from which your club (in Australia), District or Hunt Club can articulate its commitment to the safety of its members, is also able to be downloaded from the book's website and we welcome feedback so we can keep it up to date. Giveaways in electronic form include:

   a.   A generic equestrian organisation risk management policy, framework and plan which uses as its start point, the International Standards Organisation's ISO 31000, risk management—principles and guidelines. It includes generic taskings for typical organisation structures as a start point or a comparison resource for your organisation's risk management of equestrian mounted games. Note that this suite of documents is designed as a start point and you should feel free to disregard all or any of it if it is not useful but, in the hope that some of it will be of use, it is offered as a considered start point.

   b.   An Excel spreadsheet that is generated by my risk management company's risk management tool is also offered which shows an auditable trail of threats to the activity's success, envisaged risk events and the controls suggested to counter the threats/risks to the activity. The four sheets provide:

      (1) a summary of the risks identified by category at the risk profile tab,

      (2) an assumption report that lists all the assumptions identified that may need to be tested to ensure that the controls envisaged will actually provide the desired effect,

      (3) a risk analysis summary that shows the risk assessment and the associated risk control taskings, and

      (4) a post activity report to prompt the analysis of the effectiveness of the risk controls immediately after the activity has been conducted with a view to improving the activity the next time it is conducted.

133. A Regional Championship organisational checklist is also offered to assist in the consideration of the organisational steps that you may like to consider if you are thrown in the deep end and have to organise a championship from scratch.

MOUNTED GAMES LESSON PLAN # 1
SAFE HANDOVER/PASS-OFF

Preconditions for the lesson

1. The following preconditions are required to deliver a safe equestrian mounted games lesson:

   a. The area for the lesson is well defined and suitable for the game being taught.

   b. There are no trip hazards or sharp objects that could increase either the likelihood or the consequences associated with a fall or slip.

   c. There is no excessive background noise which could interrupt safety related communication.

   d. Equipment is serviceable and free of splinters or sharp edges.

   e. It is desirable, though not necessary, to have a demonstration rider or a video to show riders the right way and the traps for the game.

The Lesson

2. **Lesson Objectives.** The main objectives for this lesson are:

   a. maintenance of team and individual safety spaces at all times during the lesson,

   b. outgoing and incoming rider safe cushioning techniques during the handover, and

   c. incoming rider turn and halt drill after the handover before a controlled and quiet left rein walk back to the rest of the team.

3. **Preliminaries.**

   a. Meet the riders and their ponies and ascertain experience levels of both ponies and riders.

   b. Brief any local safety or control requirements for the lesson, such as boundaries, any hand signals to be used to muster the lesson, and that a whistle blast means all activity is to stop immediately.

c. **Revision.** Confirm riding seat alternatives and when they would be used:

   (1) upright seat is used in control zones to provide maximum control of the mount with soft hands, seat and voice aids (maintain a line—ear, shoulder, hip and ankle);

   (2) three point seat is used to transition a pony up to two point seat or back to the upright seat or when in a control zone and confident of the pony's control (maintain a slightly more forward line of shoulder, knee, toe, ensuring the seat and legs retain contact with the saddle, heel is lower than the toe in the stirrup irons); and

   (3) two point seat is used to allow the pony to move freely in hoon zones (maintain the same line as for three point seat but less angle at the knee to allow the rider to clear the saddle and retain only leg pressure on the saddle with the seat above the saddle).

d. **Approach**. Explain the reason for learning. The handover is typically the most dangerous part of a game if it is executed poorly. Riders need to understand the component parts of the handover drill so that each rider is able to commence their run on their optimal/preferred line while the remainder of the riders in the team keep themselves and their mounts safely at a distance suitable for the conditions.

4. **Body of the Lesson**. Explain the three stages the lesson will take:

a. the team orientation and spacing before, during and after the game;

b. outgoing rider's responsibilities; and

c. incoming rider's responsibilities.

5. **Stage 1. Team Orientation**. The first action in teaching handover drills is to describe in detail the team's position in relation to the start box. Considerations for this first part of the handover drill are:

a. All four riders[1] should be in line abreast facing up the games arena, positioned a minimum of 10m (preferably 15m) back from the start line with the ponies as close as is safe (well drilled teams have their mounts almost stirrup to stirrup). The team will be positioned at the left rear of the lane (but not in the neighbouring lane) as viewed from behind the team, looking down the field of play. Confirm this position as the ready position and have the riders see the safety space either side of their team as it lines up. Confirm this is how the team is to be lined up before,

---

1   Depending on how many riders are in the lesson you might like to have up to five riders per team; after that it becomes slow and unwieldy.

during and after the game until the riders are asked to leave the arena (they then do so in a disciplined line abreast).

b. When the game is in play, incoming riders need to reposition themselves on the left of the line by moving in front and to the left of the team (not getting in the way of the next rider to come up to the line). As the new rider approaches their place at the left of the line, the remainder of the team waiting should leg yield to the right one horse width to make room for the new rider to re-join the line while maintaining the team's safety space.

6. **Stage 2. Outgoing Rider's Responsibilities**. Have riders view a specific demonstration if possible, noting that ideally you would have two experienced rider/pony combinations to demonstrate the techniques and safety aspects. If you don't have these available to you, consider conducting your first handover practice for outgoing riders with the riders receiving a piece of equipment (any sort will do) from you, on the ground, as you move towards them and they ride past. Then have riders perform the outgoing rider's part of the handover drill with an incoming rider. Individual corrections may be required and perhaps repetitive practice. Teaching considerations are:

a. The pony should be positioned to the rear of the changeover box so it adopts the best line for the first part of the race.

b. With the pony under control, the move forward needs to be judged and timed so that it is straight and forward at walk or trot, with head and hindquarters parallel to the lane so that both riders meet about 2m back from the start line[2]. The rider must be prepared to quickly adjust (with indirect rein or lower leg) the pony's orientation to that of a straight spine if it tries to move its hindquarters or shoulders off the line required for a safe, straight handover[3].

c. When the pony is moving straight the rider takes a one-handed (left-handed) grip on the reins and, again, must be prepared to quickly adjust (with indirect rein on the neck or lower leg), the pony's orientation if it tries to move its hindquarters or shoulders off the required line.

---

2   I prefer to have the handovers occur at 2m short of the start line as it gives the riders a little flexibility to adjust their advance if the incoming pony slows quicker than expected. Any further back than 2m gives the opposition a sizeable head start.

3   This is less likely to happen if the outgoing mount is moving freely forward (good timing/judgement) into the handover rather than being restrained when it knows it is about to be put into canter and a two point seat.

d. Riders must ensure the right hand is 45 degrees forward (to the front right of the rider), elbow bent to allow the cushion (backwards movement of the arm while the pony is moving forward) to take the equipment, ensuring their hand is outside the vertical line of the right stirrup.

Note: Neither rider conducting the handover should ride into the handover with their arm fully stretched either to the front (hand near the pony's ear) or to the side (90 degrees from the line of movement). Of these options, the former is by far the most dangerous as it brings the riders much too close for comfort and safety. The latter limits the cushion effect (increasing potential for injury) and gives no flexibility for the rider to chase the handover if one or both ponies move away from the handover at the last instant.

e. Fingers need to be fully stretched/extended with the hand open. The outgoing rider has a responsibility to provide the incoming rider with as big a target as possible. The outgoing rider should try not to have their hand move up and down in the vertical plane as it makes it very hard to place the equipment accurately while moving.

f. The outgoing rider takes a firm, full-handed grip of the equipment while taking the arm to the rear (cushion), watching the equipment until it is confirmed as secure in their grip.

g. The rider then looks to the first task and adjusts the line early, if necessary, to maximise the chance of success at the first task in the field of play in the race.

7. **Stage 3. Incoming Rider Responsibilities.** Provide another demonstration of the handover, if possible, this time focusing on the incoming rider's responsibilities. Have riders imitate the incoming rider's part of the handover drill. Individual corrections may be required and perhaps repetitive practice. Teaching considerations are:

a. The incoming rider must have their mount under control to effect a safe handover. Both riders are responsible for the safe handover/conduct of the game and if either rider feels the handover has potential to hurt either riders or ponies they must abort the handover and yield their mount away from potential danger.

b. The equipment should be held and offered so it can be taken by the outgoing rider with minimum adjustment in their hand to do their first task with the equipment. For example, in the Five Flag/Flag Fliers race, the incoming rider should offer the flag/cane by holding it close to the flag, it must be vertical (especially to avoid an eye injury), as this allows the outgoing rider to grasp the cane where they like so they do not have to adjust their grip to place the flag in the cone after their hoon zone.

c. A fingertip grip on the equipment by the incoming rider is required, regardless of what equipment is being handed over. This allows the outgoing rider to take the equipment even if at the last moment the incoming rider has tensed up as a result of excitement or an unexpected movement by their pony.

d. The incoming rider needs to control their pony with one hand for the handover, starting with the transition down, cushioning the handover, then turning and stopping. This manoeuvre is made more complex as better teams strive to maintain momentum during the handover but, at the same time, to position the incoming rider to be able to recover quickly if the equipment is accidentally dropped.

e. If a hoon zone precedes the handover, the incoming rider will have to transition down from their two point seat to a three point seat then to an upright seat to effect the handover. The reins should only be transferred to the left hand after the three point seat has been achieved and the rider is preparing for the upright-seated transition down.

f. As already practiced in the outgoing riders' drill, riders must ensure the right hand is 45 degrees forward (to the front right of the rider), elbow bent to cushion the act of taking the equipment, ensuring their hand is outside the vertical line of the right stirrup.

g. For safety reasons, riders may need to be reminded not to ride into the handover with the arm fully stretched either to the front or to the side. Both these options risk injury to the riders and may limit the flexibility to complete the handover successfully if either pony moves unexpectedly as the handover is being attempted.

h. The reins should be held one-handed such that the rider can exert pressure on the right rein to effect a right turn as the handover is being effected, while the rider is both sitting deep and looking back to confirm the outgoing rider has the equipment. The right turn aid is supported by the movement of the incoming rider's hips as the rider looks back to confirm the handover's success.

i. The incoming rider must be prepared for recovery if equipment is dropped.

j. After the outgoing pony has left the changeover box it is important that the incoming pony settles quickly for the next task. The pony should stop and stand, albeit momentarily, before its efforts are rewarded. Once stationary, the pony can be patted gently on the lower neck near the withers to emphasise positive encouraging feedback and this can be supported with a gentle/reassuring voice aid.

k. The pony should then be turned to the left and walked back to the remainder of the team, if possible on a long rein. On joining the line, the rider should refocus on the game and be prepared to offer instructions to the rider in play who will usually have only a limited view of the game unfolding around them.

8. **Confirmation.** Present a race scenario to confirm the lesson's objectives have been met and to bring it together for the riders. Praise good efforts and ensure that all are concentrating on achieving both team and individual safety spaces.

9. **Conclusion.**

a. Clear up doubtful points.

b. Provide a summary on the group's achievements.

c. Confirm the relevance of the lesson.

d. Preview the next lesson (assuming one is planned).

e. Dismiss the group.

MOUNTED GAMES LESSON PLAN # 2 FIVE FLAG/FLAG FLIERS

Preconditions for the lesson

1. The following preconditions are required to deliver a safe equestrian mounted games lesson:
    a. The area for the lesson is well defined and suitable for the game being taught.
    b. There are no trip hazards or sharp objects that could increase either the likelihood or the consequences associated with a fall or slip.
    c. There is no excessive background noise which could interrupt safety related communication.
    d. Equipment is serviceable and free of splinters or sharp edges.
    e. It is desirable, though not necessary, to have a demonstration rider or a video to show riders the right way and the traps for the game.

The lesson

2. **Introduction.** Five Flag/Flag Fliers requires two road cones with the top cut off to produce a 10cm/4 in hole. The cones are placed on the middle line of the lane, with one on the centreline and the other 2m behind the changeover line. The five flags are 120cm/4ft canes with a flag secured at the top of the cane. The first rider starts the race with one flag and the remaining four are placed in the cone on the centreline with the flags arranged the same way for all teams.

3. **Lesson Objectives.** The main objectives for this lesson are that the riders:
    a. understand the rules of the game;
    b. understand the safety implications associated with handing over the flag;
    c. can ride efficient lines to the far cone and place the flag in the cone such that it does not impede subsequent riders;
    d. can draw a flag from the middle cone with minimum disturbance to the remaining flags; and

    e. demonstrate safe handovers of the equipment including confirmation of the handover lesson objectives.

4. **Preliminaries.**

    a. Meet the riders and their ponies and ascertain experience levels of both ponies and riders.

    b. Brief any local safety or control requirements for the lesson, such as boundaries, any hand signals to be used to muster the lesson, and that a whistle blast means all activity is to stop immediately.

    c. **Revision**. Confirm handover drills and safety space requirements.

    d. **Approach**. Explain the reason for learning. Commonly you will need to advise/remind the team members that the game will be played at an upcoming competition or championship and that it is in their best interests to learn and practice the best way to play the game for the safety and enjoyment of both rider and pony. Five Flag/Flag Fliers also has a particular requirement for riders to be conscious of the need to finish their leg of the race with the equipment placed in a specific way to enhance the likelihood of successful completion by the following team riders.

5. **Body of the Lesson.** The lesson will comprise four stages. They are:

    a. description of the game and confirmation of the rules,

    b. practice of the outward leg of the race,

    c. practice of the homeward leg of the race, and

    d. visualisation of the race.

6. **Stage 1. Description and Confirmation of the Rules for the Game.**

    a. Refer directly to the rule book.

    b. Describe the component parts of the game.

        (1) The first 60m is a hoon zone, which requires a two point seat and correct hold on the flag.

        (2) The turnaround point at the far cone requires a transition down, the pony to be turned, with the hold on the flag changed before it is placed in the cone.

        (3) The 25m from the far cone to the centre cone can be a hoon zone to approach and pluck the flag, though less experienced riders may need to transition to a control zone prior to plucking the flag.

        (4) The flag is handed over to the next rider.

c. Explain the techniques to be used in the hoon and control zones. Using the demonstration rider, have them demonstrate the game from handover to handover with riders concentrating on the line to the turnaround point, the placement technique and the flag pluck technique.

7. **Stage 2. Practice the Outward Part of the Race.** Have riders imitate the outward part of the race. Individual corrections may be required and perhaps repetitive/individual practice (a cone per rider will speed up practice if sufficient space and cones are available). Coaches commonly need to confirm the following elements:

a. The rider starts the race or takes the handover (right-handed) holding the flag in the middle of the cane or closer to the end with the pony adopting a right rein canter (offside foreleg leading). The hand holds the cane between the thumb and forefinger and the remaining fingers grasp the right rein.

b. Reins should be held with two hands for as long as possible.

c. With the rider in a two point seat, the flag is held steady so that it does not distract the pony and is held ready for placing in the far cone.

d. In the two point seat the rider should have a straight back, heels low, head up and be looking ahead.

e. About 5m to 10m short of the turnaround point the rider should come back to three point seat, or upright position if greater control is required. The rider takes a left-handed grip on both reins, with the left hand able to apply pressure on the right rein to achieve the right turnaround in the vicinity of the cone, and then turns the pony either at a slow canter or a trot.

f. To place the flag in the cone the rider bends forward at the hips to keep the combined centre of gravity close to the pony. Riders need to be careful that pressure from the left leg does not push a well-trained pony onto the cone.

g. The rider adjusts the hold on the cane to align with the pointed index finger and, with the cane pressed against the forearm for stability, places the flag in the cone. When placing the flag the rider aims for an imaginary point in the middle of the 'target.'

h. The flag is left in the cone laying back, pointing down the arena, to keep it out of the way of subsequent team members. Remember, the aim is to make the game easier for the next rider wherever possible.

8.   **Stage 3. Practice the Homeward Part of the Race.** Have riders imitate the homeward part of the race. Individual corrections may be required and perhaps repetitive/individual practice. Practice with individual cones and flags if space permits[4]. Coaches commonly need to confirm the following elements:

a.   The two point seat is used in the 25m hoon zone to approach the cone and flags in the middle of the lane.

b.   Depending on the location of the remaining flag, a 'dink' may be required (rider and pony describe an 'S' in front of the cone and as they pass it, in order to bring the pony past the equipment on a slightly longer line, giving the rider a little more time to execute the flag pluck).

c.   The flag is plucked with the thumb, forefinger and middle finger (as shown in support photographs in the online resources) and, at the same time, lifting the flag up and away from the remaining flags in the cone.

d.   Avoid a heavy-handed or back-handed pull of the flag. This may work well when riders are young and going slow but such techniques will let them down when they become faster and more competent on their pony. The rider needs to take care not to knock/push the remaining flags together as this will slow down the next rider who will have to separate them to draw only one flag.

e.   The flag is twirled once through the fingers (by rotating the wrist anti-clockwise 45 degrees and straightening the middle finger, then adjusting the grip and repositioning in a fingertip grasp) to take the handover hold. Only a single twirl of the flag is needed to adopt the handover hold. Some riders become excited and extravagant and do multiple twirls but this should be discouraged as it increases the likelihood of a fumble before the handover.

9.   **Stage 4. Visualise the Game.** Riders need to be coached to visualise the component parts of the race and the actions required at the equipment. Riders should be prepared to describe the riding requirements of the race as well as the equipment techniques used in the control zones.

a.   Riders should visualise the following elements: outgoing handover, their line of approach to the far cone, the 60m hoon zone to the far cone, placement of the flag, the 25m hoon zones to the central cone and then to the handover, their control zones, the flag pluck, and the incoming handover.

---

4   If using parents to help position and reposition equipment, try to have them help children other than their own. This is often easier on the riders (and parents)!

b. The rider visualises taking the handover (right-handed) and holding the flag in the middle of the cane or closer to the end, adopting a two point seat, and riding at least a metre wide of the cone at the turnaround point and a little past it.

c. The rider visualises coming back to three point seat just short of the turnaround point, turning the mount, adjusting the hold on the cane, placing the flag in the cone and laying the flag back, pointing down the lane, to keep it away from other riders.

d. The rider then visualises adopting a two point seat for about 20m, then a three point seat to control the approach to the flags in the cone at the middle of the lane[5]. The flag is twirled once through the fingers after being picked up to take the handover hold. The right-handed handover technique is used to hand over the flag.

10. **Confirmation.** Present a race scenario to confirm the lesson and bring it together for the riders. Praise good points and don't worry if some techniques have not come easily to riders.

11. **Conclusion.**

a. Clear up doubtful points.

b. Provide a summary on the group's achievements.

c. Confirm the relevance of the lesson.

d. Preview the next lesson (assuming one is planned).

e. Dismiss the group.

---

5   Depending on the size of the pony or the orientation of the flags it might be prudent for the rider to dink before the middle cone to give him/her a little more time with the equipment without losing momentum in the race. A well drilled and experienced rider will make the decision on their outward journey past the middle cone regarding what line to approach the middle cone on their return, as the lay of the flags will dictate the best approach.

MOUNTED GAMES LESSON PLAN # 3
HI/LO/HILO

Preconditions for the lesson

1. The following preconditions are required to deliver a safe equestrian mounted games lesson:
   a. The area for the lesson is well defined and suitable for the game being taught.
   b. There are no trip hazards or sharp objects that could increase either the likelihood or the consequences associated with a fall or slip.
   c. There is no excessive background noise which could interrupt safety related communication.
   d. Equipment is serviceable and free of splinters or sharp edges.
   e. It is desirable, though not necessary, to have a demonstration rider or a video to show riders the right way and the traps for the game.

The lesson

2. **Introduction.** Refer to the relevant rule book for equipment and placement requirements. Generally, however, five tennis balls, four standard road cones and a stand with a ball catching bag at 2.1m/7ft above the ground are required.

3. **Lesson Objectives.** The main objectives for this lesson are that the riders:
   a. understand the rules of the game;
   b. understand the safety implications associated with handing over the equipment;
   c. can ride efficient lines to the stand at the far end and place the ball in the net;
   d. can ride under control to the cone;
   e. can pick up a ball with the thumb at the rear (back door closed) and a rearwards lifting motion; and
   f. can execute a safe handover.

4. **Preliminaries.**

   a. Meet the riders and their ponies and ascertain experience levels of both ponies and riders.

   b. Brief any local safety or control requirements for the lesson, such as boundaries, any hand signals to be used to muster the lesson, and that a whistle blast means all activity is to stop immediately.

   c. **Revision.** Confirm handover drills and safety space requirements.

   d. **Approach.** Explain the reason for learning. Commonly you will need to advise/remind the team members that the game will be played at an upcoming competition or championship and that it is in their best interests to learn and practice the best way to play the game for the safety and enjoyment of both rider and pony.

5. **Body of the Lesson.** Explain the four stages the lesson will take:

   a. description of the game and confirmation of the rules,

   b. practice of the outward leg of the race,

   c. practice of the homeward leg of the race, and

   d. visualisation of the race.

6. **Stage 1. Description and Confirmation of the Rules for the Game.**

   a. Refer directly to the rule book.

   b. Describe the component parts of the game.

      (1) The first 60m is a hoon zone, which requires a two point seat to the ball catching bag at the turnaround point.

      (2) The turnaround point requires a transition down, with the pony to be turned either behind or in front of the bag, and the ball to be placed in the bag.

      (3) The rider then approaches one of the four cones along the middle line, usually employing a dink, and picks up another ball. The preferred order for picking up the balls from the cones is confirmed before the game begins, but needs to be flexible if a rider cannot pick up their designated ball.

      (4) The ball is handed over to the next rider.

   c. Using the demonstration rider, have them demonstrate the game from handover to handover with riders concentrating on the line to the ball catching bag and their line away from it in preparation for picking up their designated ball, and their technique for the ball pick-up.

7. **Stage 2. Practice the Outward Part of the Race**. Have riders imitate the outward part of the race. Individual corrections may be required and perhaps repetitive/individual practice. Coaches commonly need to confirm the following elements:

    a. Decide whether the rider's line will take them in front of the bag or behind it (generally bigger horses will be more balanced turning behind the bag while some smaller horses and ponies can turn in front and not interfere with the stand).

    b. From the start or handover, have the rider ride the hoon zone to the bag with two hands on the reins, using the best line possible for the pony and rider combination. This should be in a two point seat letting the pony trot, canter or gallop freely, about 1m to 2m from the line of cones along the middle line of the lane. The width from the line of cones on the middle line will usually be dictated by the skill level of the rider and pony.

    c. The first control zone starts when the rider backs off the speed of approach and adopts the three point or upright seated position before turning their mount at or around the bag.

    d. When placing the ball in the bag from behind, I like to have my riders ride slightly (1.5m to 2m) beyond the bag. They then execute a two-handed turn and demand a close line to the pole, with two hands on the reins, then ride the pony in a straight line that will pass the bag, adopt a one-handed rein contact with the cavalry/stockman grip on the reins with the non-master hand and place the ball in the bag with the master hand. If turning in front of the pole the rider adopts the one-handed grip just before the pole when halted or during the controlled turn.

    e. The lower legs are used to keep the pony close to the pole when placing the ball in the bag, while turning in front or behind it. The pony should not be allowed to drift into the pole or too far away so that the rider has to risk a throw (never a high percentage option) or go around again, thereby losing time. The turn should be controlled with the reins and legs. If the pony tends to bend its neck and not turn the rest of its body, a firm outside rein against the neck and the rider sitting up straight, with hips turned in the direction to be taken, will assist the pony to turn.

8. **Stage 3. Practice the Homeward Part of the Race.** Have riders imitate the homeward part of the race. Individual corrections may be required and perhaps repetitive/individual practice. Coaches may wish to confirm the following elements:

    a. After placing the ball in the bag, the pony is drifted to the correct line for the planned pick-up with the rider's master hand.

b. A dink may need to be employed. It is generally true that the taller the pony, the deeper the dink required, but this is dependent on the skill of the rider. Riders on bigger horses or those who are very new to games riding must be prepared to stop to pick the ball up if necessary.

c. The rider should check the pony's forward momentum momentarily with a half halt before leaning down, and slightly forward, in preparation for picking up the ball off the cone.

d. A good pick-up requires the forehand technique and a big back-lift to keep the hands 'soft'. The rider should prepare for the pick-up by having the master hand raised above the height of the ball on the cone, and the fingers stretched and apart with the thumb in line with the middle finger but pointing down towards the ground. As the mount moves past the cone the arm is brought down onto the ball with the fingers to the front and the thumb at back of the ball. A high back-lift motion completes the pick-up.

e. The rider should not snatch at the ball to pick it up or use a dragging back-handed motion to attempt to pick up the ball. The backhand technique will become a liability as the rider gets better and faster on larger horses.

f. The non-master hand should be holding the reins in a single-handed active grip (so that the pony feels the rider's presence through the reins), ensuring the pony does not drift onto the cone or away from the optimum line. Lower legs should not put uneven pressure on the sides of the pony as this may be interpreted as an aid to move away from, or to/onto, the cone.

g. Once the ball is securely in the hand, the reins are held in a two-handed bridge, with the ball held in the thumb and forefinger and the remaining fingers applying the lightest pressure necessary on the reins and the hoon zone is ridden to the changeover control zone.

h. Upon entering this final control zone for the race, the rider should adopt the single-handed grip on the reins and adjust the grip on the ball so that they hold it in their fingertips in order to present the ball for the outgoing rider to grab with a full-handed grip.

i. Complete the handover drill as described in Lesson #1.

9. **Stage 4. Visualise the Game.** Riders need to be coached to visualise the component parts of the race and the actions required at the equipment. Riders should be prepared to describe the riding requirements of the race as well as the techniques to be used at the bag and at the pick-up point.

a. Riders should visualise the following elements: the handover to start their run, lines of approach to the bag and to the cone to pick up the next ball, location/ length of the hoon zones and control zones, and the handover to the next rider.

b. The rider should visualise riding the hoon zone to the bag with two hands on the reins, and the line they will take to the bag.

c. They should see themselves approaching the bag coming back to a three point or upright seat, depending on their level of ability, as they turn their pony around or in front of the bag.

d. The rider should visualise the ball being dropped into the bag and the line they will take as they ride away from the bag towards the cone where they will pick up the next ball.

e. They will then execute a dink and pick up the ball smoothly, visualising the fingers spread and the thumb at the back of the hand in line with the middle finger to secure the ball with the 'closed back door'. The hand is brought down from above and in front of the ball, followed by a high back-lift making the pick-up soft and leaving the cone undisturbed.

f. The rider then visualises a safe handover and turning to face back down the lane as the outgoing rider departs.

10. **Confirmation.** Conduct a confirmatory race to test that the lesson's objectives have been achieved. Focus on the good points, noting that new skills and techniques will take time to be mastered and refined.

11. **Conclusion.**

a. Clear up doubtful points.

b. Provide a summary on the group's achievements.

c. Confirm the relevance of the lesson.

d. Preview the next lesson (assuming one is planned).

e. Dismiss the group.

MOUNTED GAMES LESSON PLAN # 4
STEPPING STONE DASH/AGILITY ACES

Preconditions for the lesson

1. The following preconditions are required to deliver a safe equestrian mounted games lesson:

   a. The area for the lesson is well defined and suitable for the game being taught.

   b. There are no trip hazards or sharp objects that could increase either the likelihood or the consequences associated with a fall or slip.

   c. There is no excessive background noise which could interrupt safety related communication.

   d. Equipment is serviceable and stable and can take the weight of the heaviest participant moving over the equipment with all their weight on one foot. The stepping stone or pot should be made stable by removing or flattening tufts of grass beneath them to reduce the likelihood of the equipment tipping as the rider steps or runs on it.

   e. It is desirable, though not necessary, to have a demonstration rider or a video to show riders the right way and the traps for the game.

The lesson

2. **Introduction**. Refer to the relevant rule book for equipment and placement requirements. Generally, however, six stepping stones or upturned pots are required to be placed on the middle line of the lane, with three stones/pots either side of the centreline at 60cm/2ft intervals, measured from centre to centre of each stepping stone or pot.

3. **Lesson Objectives**. The main objectives for this lesson are that the riders:

   a. understand the rules of the game;

    b. understand the safety implications associated with leading a pony unmounted at the run;

    c. can ride efficient lines to and through the race;

    d. can dismount and re mount under control ; and

    e. can execute a safe handover 'on the fly': i.e. a changeover executed at speed, where no equipment needs to be handed over to the outgoing rider.

4. **Preliminaries.**

    a. Meet the riders and their ponies and ascertain experience levels of both ponies and riders.

    b. Brief any local safety or control requirements for the lesson, such as boundaries, any hand signals to be used to muster the lesson, and that a whistle blast means all activity is to stop immediately.

    c. **Revision.** Confirm handover drills and safety space requirements.

    d. **Approach.** Explain the reason for learning. Commonly you will need to advise/ remind the team members that the game will be played at an upcoming competition or championship and that it is in their best interests to learn and practice the best way to play the game for the safety and enjoyment of both rider and pony. The Stepping Stone Dash/Agility Aces is also particularly good for practicing the moving dismount, leading the pony and the running vault.

5. **Body of the Lesson**. Explain the three stages the lesson will take:

    a. description of the game and confirmation of the rules,

    b. practice the component parts of the race, and

    c. visualisation of the race.

6. **Stage 1. Description and Confirmation of the Rules for the Game**. Each rider in the Stepping Stone Dash/Agility Aces rides a single length of the playing field, negotiating the equipment in one direction only, with the first and third riders starting from the start/finish line, and the second and fourth riders starting from the changeover line.

    a. Refer directly to the rule book.

    b. The component parts of the game are:

        (1) the start/changeover,

        (2) the dismount,

        (3) controlling the pony in-hand,

        (4) negotiating the stepping stones,

(5) the remount, and

(6) ride across the changeover line (first and third riders) or the start/finish line (second and fourth riders).

c. Using the demonstration rider, have them demonstrate the game from start to changeover. Riders should concentrate on the techniques for the dismount, crossing the stones and the remount, as well as the line to be ridden after remounting to cross the changeover line.

7. **Stage 2. Practice the Component Parts of the Race.**

a. **Start/changeover.** The first rider starts the race in the same way as all other races. Timing of subsequent handovers, however, is very important for both experienced and inexperienced teams. All four of the incoming pony's hooves must be in the changeover box before the outgoing pony enters the field of play and this requires fine judgement, especially as the riders become faster with experience. As no equipment is changing hands outgoing riders can be trained to enter the field of play with controlled momentum.

Note: Some countries insist the rider enters the changeover box and have their pony immobile before allowing their forward movement into the handover. In this case correct timing of the forward movement is critical to an efficient handover.

b. **Dismount.** The dismount location will be dictated by the time it will take the dismounted rider to get full control of line and speed of the led pony. The better controlled/trained the pony, the closer to the stones the dismount can be. On the other hand, the dismount location can be relatively close to the start/changeover line depending on the rider's experience and speed across the ground when dismounted.

(1) **Inexperienced teams/riders.** Inexperienced teams will maximise the speed and ground covering ability of their pony in the 20m hoon zone before dismounting close to the stepping stones and slightly to the right of the middle line of the lane.

(2) **Experienced teams/riders.** Riders in experienced teams will ensure they have selected a line that sees them able to dismount and run so that they require minimal line adjustment and, once on the ground, successfully negotiate the stepping stones.

c.   **Controlling the Pony in-hand.**

(1) Once on the ground it is very important that the pony is controlled with only the nearside rein.

(2) Riders should hold the rein close to the bit with the upper arm parallel to the ground so that the elbow is able to touch the pony's neck should it try to push in on the rider. The forearm is horizontal and facing the direction of movement with the wrist twisted towards the pony's neck also. This gives the rider sufficient control to bring the pony onto the correct line without it pushing the rider off their line.

(3) It is very important that the elbow does not rise above/over the line of the neck to avoid any perception that the pony is assisting the dismounted rider to maintain balance and momentum, as this may result in the team being eliminated.

d.   **Negotiating the Stones**.

(1) The rider should ensure that the whole foot hits the top of the stones and that no part of the foot is perceived to have slipped off the stone.

(2) As the rider is negotiating the fourth and fifth stones the leading arm should be extended to push the pony marginally in front of the rider to ensure the saddle is close to the rider when they step off the sixth/last stone.

(3) The experienced rider needs to know how many steps they require after crossing the stones before they can vault with balance and precision, as this will dictate which foot needs to be first on the stones and, consequently, which will be last on the stones. This calculation will depend on how the rider likes to vault (i.e. with a two footed bounce, or a dominant left foot bounce, or just a left foot skip with a high right leg lift).

(4) If the equipment is moved by either the pony or the rider stumbling over the stones, if the rider does not step on any stone, or if their foot slips off a stone, the rider must replace any disturbed stones and then renegotiate all six stepping stones in the correct order. The team will be eliminated if the rider fails to do this.

e.   **Remount**.

(1) The remount/vault should be executed without putting pressure on either rein as a well-trained pony will respond to that pressure and turn away from the optimum line.

(2) Inexperienced riders will lead their pony as they cross the stepping stones on

foot then, using their stirrup, mount and ride to the changeover line to allow the next rider to enter the race.

(3) Experienced riders will aim to vault onto their pony after their first step off the stepping stones has hit the ground and, once in the saddle, ensure that they are not going to interrupt the line of the next rider as they attempt a well-timed changeover with momentum.

f. **Crossing the Changeover and Start/Finish Lines.**

(1) Riders must be in the saddle facing forwards when crossing out of the field of play. It is also very important that the incoming rider has sufficient control of their mount to stay clear of the outgoing rider's preferred line.

(2) Experienced riders will ride to the changeover line in a three point seat, often not having recovered their stirrups after vaulting onto their pony. It is very important for the incoming rider to be balanced as soon as possible after the remount/vault, as they need to ensure that they maintain a safe distance from the outgoing rider as they execute the flying changeover.

(3) Immediately upon leaving the field of play it is important to transition down safely from the faster gait to the trot, walk and halt/stop. This race is one of the fastest at the highest levels and it is very important that all incoming riders turn their ponies to the right if they are not able to stop their pony before it reaches the rider who has not yet ridden, or has completed, their leg of the race.

(4) Likewise, it is important that safety spaces include space behind the standing ponies so other teams' ponies can pass between the rear of the team and the fencing/bunting defining the arena. Settling the pony after the race is important to get it ready for the next race.

8. **Stage 3. Visualise the Race.** Riders should visualise the following elements: the initial changeover as they enter the field of play, the line of approach to the stepping stones, the hoon zones and control zones, the planned dismount and remount/vault locations, the actions they need to take if they make any error at the equipment, and their line to and after the changeover.

9. **Confirmation.** Conduct a confirmatory race to give all riders a feel for the complexities of what appears to be a simple race when the component parts are completed quickly and effectively. Depending on the experience and skill of the team's members the race can be conducted in several ways. For example:

a. Inexperienced teams will maximise the speed and ground covering ability of their pony in the 20m hoon zone before dismounting close to the stepping stones, slightly to the right of the line of stones. They will then lead their pony as they cross the stepping stones then, using their stirrup, mount and ride to the changeover line to allow the next rider to enter the race.

b. Experienced riders will ensure they have selected a line that allows them to dismount and run with minimal or no line adjustment to successfully negotiate the stepping stones. They will vault onto their ponies after their first step off the sixth stepping stone has hit the ground and, once in the saddle, they will ensure that they do not obstruct the planned line of the next rider as they execute a well-judged and well-timed changeover at speed.

10. **Conclusion.**

   a. Clear up doubtful points.

   b. Provide a summary on the group's achievements.

   c. Confirm the relevance of the lesson.

   d. Preview the next lesson (assuming one is planned).

   e. Dismiss the group.

MOUNTED GAMES LESSON PLAN # 5
TACK SHOP

Preconditions for the lesson

1. The following preconditions are required to deliver a safe equestrian mounted games lesson:

   a. The area for the lesson is well defined and suitable for the game being taught.

   b. There are no trip hazards or sharp objects that could increase either the likelihood or the consequences associated with a fall or slip.

   c. There is no excessive background noise which could interrupt safety related communication.

   d. Equipment is serviceable and free of splinters or sharp edges. You may need to adjust the equipment if it is a very windy day as pieces of equipment blown off a stand in front of a green pony can pose a considerable impediment to the pony's training! Alternatively, consider training for the race when the weather is more accommodating for achievement of the lesson objectives.

   e. It is desirable, though not necessary, to have a demonstration rider or a video to show rider the right way and the traps for the game.

The lesson

2. **Introduction.** Refer to the relevant rule book for equipment and placement requirements. Generally, however, a coin stand is placed in the middle of the lane 15m from the start/finish line (the '1/4 line'), a drum or table is placed 15m from the changeover line (the '3/4 line') with an empty tack box on it, and another drum is placed 3m behind the changeover line with a sponge, tail bandage, tin of saddle soap and a dandy brush. The first rider starts with a plyboard coin to place in the tray on the coin stand.

3. **Lesson Objectives**. The main objectives for this lesson are that the riders:

   a. understand the rules of the game;

   b. understand the safety implications associated with turning around the fifth rider who participates, unmounted, in this game;

   c. can ride efficient lines to all equipment;

   d. can ride under control at all times;

   e. understand the requirements of the fifth rider on the ground in order to ensure equipment is placed in the tack box in the optimum manner; and

   f. can execute a safe handover.

4. **Preliminaries.**

   a. Meet the riders and their ponies and ascertain experience levels of both ponies and riders.

   b. Brief any local safety or control requirements for the lesson, such as boundaries, any hand signals to be used to muster the lesson, and that a whistle blast means all activity is to stop immediately.

   c. **Revision.** Confirm handover drills and safety space requirements.

   d. **Approach**. Explain the reason for learning. Commonly you will need to advise/remind the team members that the game will be played at an upcoming competition or championship and that it is in their best interests to learn and practice the best way to play the game for the safety and enjoyment of both rider and pony. The Tack Shop Race is one race where solid training is particularly rewarded in competition. It is a technical game that requires balanced riding and efficient lines to be ridden. The involvement of the fifth rider on the ground is critical in ensuring the equipment can be carried securely, and therefore faster, between the pick-up drum and the fifth rider, and then back to the drum again.

5. **Body of the Lesson**. Explain the five stages of the lesson which will include:

   a. description of the game and confirmation of the rules,

   b. the fifth rider's responsibilities,

   c. practice the outward leg of the race,

   d. practice the homeward leg of the race, and

   e. visualisation of the race.

6. **Stage 1. Description and Confirmation of the Rules for the Game.**

   a. Refer directly to the rule book.

b. Describe the component parts of the game:

    (1) The first rider starts with a coin which must be placed safely in the tray on the coin stand on the 1/4 line.

    (2) The next 30m to the drum on the 3/4 line is a hoon zone, followed by the pick-up of the tack box from the drum.

    (3) The turnaround point at the fifth rider and end drum requires a transition down and presentation of the tack box for the fifth rider to place an item of equipment securely in it.

    (4) The rider then replaces the tack box on the drum and rides the 30m hoon zone to the coin stand to retrieve the coin (noting that most riders will need to transition to a control zone prior to picking up the coin).

    (5) The coin is then handed over to the next rider who repeats the process.

c. A demonstration at this stage will help riders see how the race is conducted and allow them to ask questions but, as noted earlier, there are many technical aspects to performing this game well and these need to be covered in detail in each stage of the lesson.

7. **Stage 2. Describe the Fifth Rider's Responsibilities.** The fifth rider is responsible for placing one item of tack in the offered box for each rider, keeping the pony off the end drum on which the equipment has been placed, and ensuring they are not trodden on or pushed over by the incoming pony and rider. Assuming that the incoming rider is going to offer the tack box in their right hand, the fifth rider should stand one pace to the rear and one pace to the right of the drum as they look back down the arena.

    a. **Footwork of the Fifth Rider.** As the incoming rider and pony turn around the fifth rider, and the fifth rider places a piece of equipment in the tack box, the fifth rider moves in the same but smaller arc as the rider and pony, ensuring that the pony is kept away from the drum and equipment. The fifth rider does this by taking a large step with their right foot back and to the rear, following the arc of the pony, while pivoting on their left foot. This step is repeated, usually once or twice, until the pony is sent on its next intended line (towards the drum on the 3/4 line).[6]

---

6   See the supporting resources for pictures of the fifth riders executing their responsibilities.

b. **Wedging the Equipment**. The order in which the fifth rider places the equipment in the tack box is important, as the technique aims to wedge the equipment as securely as possible. This gives the riders confidence as they pick up the tack box from the 3/4 line drum and subsequently replace it, allowing them to ride faster. It is also possible that, if the tack box should fall from the drum, the contents will not be displaced, which allows a much faster recovery.

    (1) The sponge should be 'scrunched' in a one-handed grip and, as the tack box is offered by the first rider, the fifth rider places their empty hand under the box where the sponge is to be placed and then, with the other hand, the sponge is forced into the confined space so it will expand and remain wedged and stable in the box.

    (2) Using the same technique the fifth rider places/wedges the tail bandage for the second rider, then the tin of saddle soap for the third rider. The dandy brush for the last rider can usually be placed so that the sponge wedges it into place as well.

c. **Selection of the Fifth Rider.** Look for the best fifth rider in the team because a skilled fifth rider can make the race faster for the other riders by giving them confidence that the equipment is securely wedged, allowing riders to approach the control zones with greater momentum. There is considerable potential benefit if one of the team members is prepared to specialise in this position. (I always look for fifth riders with good hand/eye coordination, particularly for the fishing race where a good fifth rider with quick clean hands can win the race for your team.)

8. **Stage 3. Practice the Outward Leg of the Race.** Have riders imitate the outward leg of the race. Individual corrections may be required and perhaps repetitive/individual practice. The following elements may need to be confirmed:

a. With the coin in their master hand, the rider rides to the coin box in a two point seat and places the coin in the tray with a backwards and downwards motion. The fingers should stay on the coin momentarily at the point of impact to absorb any concussive energy and ensure it does not bounce out of the tray. (Prior to placing the coin I like to see the coin held with the thumb and little finger under the coin and the three remaining fingers on top of the coin. That way the coin can be placed with three fingers pressing down and the thumb and little finger moving outwards to release their grip at the last fraction of a second.)

b. The rider continues in the two point seat until entering the control zone for picking up the tack box from the drum on the 3/4 line. A dink—even a shallow one—will enhance the chances of a successful pick-up. As the first rider picks up an empty box they can do this with greater speed than subsequent riders, who will need to minimise the risk of items falling out of the tack box, especially if they use a heavy-handed pick-up technique.

c. Having picked up the tack box they ride to the turnaround point and present the box to the fifth rider for placement of the appropriate item.

(1) The fifth rider should advise the team members how they want the box presented to them to make this aspect of the race as effective and efficient as possible. (This will have been agreed and practiced well in advance of the race.)

(2) Ensure riders do not put the fifth rider at risk by riding a wrong line or by allowing their pony to fall inwards through the shoulder at the turnaround point.

9. **Stage 4. Practice the Homeward Leg of the Race.** Have riders imitate the homeward leg of the race. Individual corrections may be required and perhaps repetitive/individual practice. The following elements may need to be confirmed:

a. The tack box needs to be placed on the drum with a backwards and downwards movement, with a sharp back-lift once the box has been placed. This will avoid the tack box being replaced on the drum with forward momentum which may see it slide off.

b. A two point seat is used to ride the 30m hoon zone to the coin stand, where the rider needs to check the pony to bleed off the speed to ensure the coin is able to be picked up first time. I train my riders and their ponies to stop at the coin stand so that during competitions the pony is expecting to stop and will check up nicely to give the rider time to collect the coin.

(1) If a rider overshoots the coin stand, practice the rider in backing the pony unless they have travelled too far past it. The back-up is often quicker than turning the pony.

(2) Some riders may need to dink to the coin stand as the slightly greater length of time at the stand may be just enough to pick up the coin cleanly.

c. The coin is handed over to the next rider. All riders involved in the handover of the coin should agree the orientation and method of presenting the coin to maximise the likelihood of a successful handover to the outgoing rider.

10. **Stage 5. Visualise the Game.** Riders need to be coached to visualise the techniques they will need to employ throughout this race. They should be prepared to describe the riding requirements of the race as well as the equipment techniques used in the control zones. The fifth rider also needs to be able to visualise their critical part in this race.

a. Riders should visualise the following elements: the outgoing handover; their line of approach to the coin stand, the drum on the 3/4 line, the turnaround point and the fifth rider, back to the drum and to the coin stand; hoon zones and control zones; and the incoming handover.

b. The rider visualises riding past the coin stand and placing the coin in the tray with very soft hands.

c. They then visualise the line to the drum on the 3/4 line and picking up the tack box with a back-lifting motion.

d. They visualise offering the box to the fifth rider as they have asked for it and riding around the fifth rider in an efficient arc, then riding to and replacing the tack box on the drum.

e. The fifth rider visualises the approaching rider and pony and the line they will take, the tack box being offered and the item of equipment being placed in the tack box in its assigned place, with the fifth rider's empty hand underneath the box supporting it while the equipment is being wedged in place. At the same time, the fifth rider is moving their feet and body, protecting the end drum and equipment, to follow the movement of the rider and pony as they turn around the fifth rider before making their way back to return the tack box to the drum on the 3/4 line.

f. The rider should then visualise adopting a two point seat to ride to the coin stand, checking their pony in time to bleed off speed to allow for a successful collection of the coin.

g. They then visualise the effective handover of the coin to the next rider using the agreed technique for offering the coin to the outgoing rider.

11. **Confirmation**. Conduct a confirmatory race to test that the lesson's objectives have been achieved. Focus on the good points, noting that new skills and techniques will take time to be mastered and refined.

12. **Conclusion.**

a. Clear up doubtful points.

b. Provide a summary on the group's achievements.

c. Confirm the relevance of the lesson.

d. Preview the next lesson (assuming one is planned).

e. Dismiss the group.

MOUNTED GAMES LESSON PLAN # 6 OLD SOCK/SOCKS AND BUCKETS

Preconditions for the lesson

1. The following preconditions are required to deliver a safe equestrian mounted games lesson:

   a. The area for the lesson is well defined and suitable for the game being taught.

   b. There are no trip hazards or sharp objects that could increase either the likelihood or the consequences associated with a fall or slip.

   c. There is no excessive background noise which could interrupt safety related communication.

   d. Equipment is serviceable and buckets are to be free of sharp edges. During training on windy days you might like to consider weighing down the buckets so they do not move while a pony is approaching them. (This should be the exception as to train continually with weighted buckets teaches the riders poor technique).

   e. It is desirable, though not necessary, to have a demonstration rider or a video to show rider the right way and the traps for the game.

The lesson

2. **Introduction.** Refer to the relevant rule book for equipment and placement requirements. Generally, however, there are five rolled and stitched socks and one bucket with a capacity of approximately 13.5 litres or 3.5 gallons. Four socks are placed on the ground at the changeover line and the bucket is placed centrally within the lane on the centreline. The first rider starts with a sock, places it in the bucket, rides to the changeover line, dismounts and picks up another sock, and then returns to the start/finish line to hand over the sock to the next rider. The second and third riders repeat this process. The fourth rider places the fourth sock in the bucket on the outward leg, picks

up the fifth and last sock from the changeover line, and then places the fifth sock in the bucket on the return to the start/finish line.

3.   **Lesson Objectives**. The main objectives for this lesson are that the riders:

   a.   understand the rules of the game;

   b.   understand the safety implications associated with handing over the equipment, the need to stay in their own lane if vaulting, and not leaning out too far to execute the sock placement in the bucket;

   c.   can ride efficient lines to the dismount point and back to the team after remounting;

   d.   can ride under control to the bucket;

   e.   can place the sock with a back-handed releasing motion, aiming for the rear/back of the bucket; and

   f.   can execute a safe handover.

4.   **Preliminaries.**

   a.   Meet the riders and their ponies and ascertain experience levels of both ponies and riders.

   b.   Brief any local safety or control requirements for the lesson, such as boundaries, any hand signals to be used to muster the lesson, and that a whistle blast means all activity is to stop immediately.

   c.   **Revision.** Confirm handover drills and safety space requirements.

   d.   **Approach.** Explain the reason for learning. Commonly you will need to advise/ remind the team members that the game will be played at an upcoming competition or championship and that it is in their best interests to learn and practice the best way to play the game for the safety and enjoyment of both rider and pony. This race is very similar to the Ball and Bucket Race, though the ball is more challenging to place successfully in the bucket. The sock allows the practice and mastery of the placement skill prior to taking on the more demanding task of the Ball and Bucket Race.

5.   **Body of the Lesson**. The lesson will comprise four stages. They are:

   a.   description and confirmation of the rules for the game,

   b.   practice of the outward half of the race,

   c.   practice of the homeward half of the race, and

   d.   visualisation of the race.

6.   **Stage 1. Description and Confirmation of the Rules for the Game.**

   a.   Refer directly to the rule book.

   b.   Describe the component parts of the game:

(1) The first 25m is a hoon zone which requires a two point seat.

(2) The sock is then placed effectively in the bucket on the centreline.

(3) The rider then rides to the turnaround point, transitions down, dismounts to pick up another sock, and remounts.

(4) For the first three riders the 60m from the changeover line back to the start/finish line is a hoon zone, requiring a transition down to effect the handover of the sock to the outgoing rider.

(5) The fourth rider has a hoon zone to the bucket on the return, where the last sock is placed in the bucket before the rider finishes the race.

c. Using the demonstration rider, have them demonstrate the game from start to changeover. Riders should concentrate on the line of the dink to the bucket, the technique for placing the sock in the bucket, the line to be ridden to the turnaround point, the location of the dismount and remount, the technique for picking up the sock, and the line to be ridden after remounting to cross the start/finish line and effect the handover.

7. **Stage 2. Practice the Outward Leg of the Race.** Have riders imitate the outward leg of the race. Individual corrections may be required and perhaps repetitive/individual practice. The following elements may need to be confirmed:

a. The rider lines up in the handover/start box to give the best line for the commencement of the race. This is usually 1m to 2m to the right of centre in the handover box if the rider aims to dink before the bucket, and to the rear of the box.

b. The rider should enter the field of play with the sock between the thumb, index finger and the middle/large finger with the remaining two fingers maintaining a contact on the right rein to ensure the effective communication with the pony via the bit.

c. The rider adopts a line to allow for a medium-sized dink (an angle of 45 degrees) and, as the line across and in front of the bucket is being ridden, the rider should lean slightly forward and to the right, with an outstretched hand with the sock.

d. The speed and angle of approach will be dictated by the skill and amount of practice both the rider and pony have undertaken. A rider that can, during the dink in the control zone, move their seat to the right, away from the centre of their saddle, and who bends their right knee to allow the seat to be lowered somewhat on the offside of the pony, will be able to get lower, and therefore closer, to the bucket.

e. The sock should be dropped out of the back of the hand when the arm swings backwards (effectively staying stationary over the bucket), thereby imparting little or no forward momentum on the sock. The wrist should not bend either up or down as a flicking motion adds momentum to the sock and such techniques frequently lead to the sock (or ball in Ball and Bucket Race) bouncing out or knocking the bucket over.

f. Once the sock is successfully in the bucket the rider should adopt a two point seat to ride to their dismount point. Just before the dismount point the rider should transition back to the three point seat and, if considered prudent, the upright seat. The rider dismounts, confirms a line that keeps the pony off the equipment, leads it to the sock/s located on the ground and picks up the left-most sock as viewed from the approaching rider's perspective (by picking up the left-most sock the rider increases his/her ability to keep the pony from stepping on or kicking the other socks, which could slow down subsequent riders).

8. **Stage 3. Practice the Homeward Leg of the Race.** Have riders imitate the homeward leg of the race. Individual corrections may be required and perhaps repetitive/individual practice. The following elements may need to be confirmed:

a. Having picked up the sock, the rider should remount as quickly as they can ensuring that they do not lose their grip on the sock which, in Pony Club events in Australia, must be held only in the hand at all times.

b. The remount will be with or without the use of stirrups, depending on the rider's level of skill and training.

c. The first three riders return to the start/finish line in a two point seat to effect the handover.

d. The fourth rider renegotiates the bucket on the homeward journey in the same manner as the outward journey, to ensure that the last sock is securely placed in the bucket and the bucket is left upright, containing all five socks, before they exit the field of play.

9. **Stage 4. Visualise the Game.** Riders need to be coached to visualise the techniques they will need to employ throughout this race. They should be prepared to describe the riding requirements of the race as well as the equipment techniques used in the control zones.

a. Riders should visualise the following elements: outgoing handover, line of approach to the bucket, ride to the changeover line, location of dismount, keeping the pony under control while picking up the equipment, the remount (either with or without the use of the stirrups), the return to the start/finish line and preparation for the handover.

    b. They will line up in the handover/start box to give the best line for the commencement of the race and the ride to the bucket. (This line will be dictated by whether the rider intends to use a dink to place the sock in the bucket.)

    c. They should visualise the good handover with soft hands and a quick turn of the head and eyes to confirm the equipment is secure, and then back to the front to look for the next task.

    d. The rider visualises riding their chosen line to the bucket and placing the sock in the bucket by leaning slightly forward and to the right, letting the sock fall out of the back of the hand.

    e. They will visualise approaching the dismount location, kicking the stirrups out, dismounting and landing with their feet facing the direction of movement.

    f. They will pick up the sock while keeping their pony from stepping on or kicking the equipment.

    g. They will visualise the remount/vault.

    h. They will then visualise the two point seat ride to the handover and the transition down just before and during the handover.

10. **Confirmation.** Conduct a confirmatory race to test that the lesson's objectives have been achieved. Focus on the good points, noting that new skills and techniques will take time to be mastered and refined.

11. **Conclusion.**

    a. Clear up doubtful points.

    b. Provide a summary on the group's achievements.

    c. Confirm the relevance of the lesson.

    d. Preview the next lesson (assuming one is planned).

    e. Dismiss the group.

CPSIA information can be obtained
at www.ICGtesting.com
Printed in the USA
BVHW011026280319
543966BV00006B/303/P